The Maharshi and His Message

PAUL BRUNTON

Sri Ramanasramam
Tiruvannamalai 606 603
INDIA

© Sri Ramanasramam
Tiruvannamalai

Thirteenth Edition	*2002*	—	*2000 copies*
Fourteenth Edition	*2004*	—	*2000 copies*
Fifteenth Edition	*2007*	—	*2000 copies*
Sixteenth Edition	2012	—	2000 copies

CC No: 1026

ISBN: 978-81-88225-50-7

Price: ₹95/-

Published by:
V.S. Ramanan
President
SRI RAMANASRAMAM
Tiruvannamalai 606 603
Tamil Nadu, INDIA
Email : ashram@sriramanamaharshi.org
Web : www.sriramanamaharshi.org

Typeset at:
Sri Ramanasramam

Printed by:
Sudarsan Graphics
Chennai 600 017, INDIA

CONTENTS

1	INTRODUCTION	i
2	THE HILL OF THE HOLY BEACON	1
3	IN A JUNGLE HERMITAGE	41
4	TABLETS OF FORGOTTEN TRUTH	64

Introduction to the Three Chapters taken from
A Search in Secret India

Messrs. Rider & Co., of London brought out in 1934 a remarkable book with the title *A Search in Secret India*. It has passed through several impressions in a very short time and is easily the latest bestseller on India. In view of its notable success, the Editor of the *London Forum* invited the author Paul Brunton to give an outline of the cause and motives which led up to his pilgrimage to India. Mr. Brunton wrote a short interesting autobiographical note which was published in the August number of the *Forum*.

A Search in Secret India lucidly narrates the author's acquaintance with, impressions of, and relation to the Maharshi who has so influenced him. The book is at present too expensive to the ordinary Indian reader and therefore the three chapters — IX, XVI and XVII — relating to the Maharshi, are reprinted in the form of a booklet with the kind permission of the author, in order to place this most important part of the work within the reach of the reader. Of course, these chapters shine better in their original setting and are best read from *A Search in Secret India* by those who can afford it.

The author had an instinctive attraction for India and it is graphically described by himself: "The Geography master takes a long, tapering pointer and moves over to the large, varnished linen map which hangs before a half-bored class. He indicates a triangular red patch which juts down to the Equator and then makes a further attempt to stimulate the obviously lagging interest of his pupils. He begins in a thin, drawling voice and with the air of one about to make a hierophantic revelation, 'India has been called the brightest jewel in the British Crown...... .'

At once a boy with moody brow, half wrapt in reverie, gives a sudden start and draws his far-flung imagination back into the stolid, brick-walled building which constitutes his school. The sound of this word *India* falling on the tympanum of his ears, or the sight of it caught up by the optic nerve of his eyes from a printed page, carries thrilling and mysterious connotations of the unknown. Some inexplicable current of thought brings it repeatedly before him. Ever and anon he makes wild projects to go there. He plans an expedition with a school-mate who is discovered and the enterprise is reluctantly abandoned. The desire to view India never leaves the promoter of that unfortunate expedition."

With the dawn of manhood, he turns to spiritualism, joins the Theosophical Society and learns more of the East. His experiences in spiritualism convince him of the survival of the spirit after the death of the body. Then other interests and his own duties hold him. He dropped his "mystic studies and concentrated upon professional work in journalism and editing". Some years pass "until he meets unexpectedly with a man who gives a temporary but vivid life to the old ambition. For the stranger's face is dusky, his head is turbaned and he comes from the sun-steeped land of Hindustan".

He was tempted to go out and investigate the subject of *yoga*. He arrived in India in 1930, and he later visited several remarkable places but few remarkable men until some inscrutable, impelling force, which he cannot understand, but which he blindly obeys, hurries his pace so that sometimes he rushes onwards as though he were a tourist. At last he is on the train to Madras.

In Madras, he accidentally met the "Anchorite of the Adyar River" who took him later to the "Sage who never speaks". In the Sage's hermitage, a stranger, Mr. Subramanya by name, obtrudes on him and solicits his visit to his own Master Sri Ramana Maharshi of Thiruvannamalai. The obtrusion of Mr. Subramanya is amusing in its naivete and surprising in its results. The graphic description of the scene of his meeting with our author is cited here for the delectation of the reader:

> Someone draws up to my side before we reach the end of the road which is to take us into Madras. I turn my head. The yellow-robed *yogi* — for it is he — rewards me with a majestic grin. His mouth stretches almost from ear to ear, and his eyes wrinkle into narrow slits.
>
> "You wish to speak to me?" I enquire.
>
> "I do, Sir," he replies quickly and with a good accent to his English. "May I ask you what you are doing in our country?"
>
> I hesitate before this inquisitiveness, and decide to give a vague reply.
>
> "Oh! Just travelling around."
>
> "You are interested in our holy men, I believe?"
>
> "Yes, a little."
>
> "I am a *yogi*, Sir," he informs me.
>
> He is the heftiest looking *yogi* I have ever seen.
>
> "How long have you been one?"
>
> "Three years, Sir."
>
> "Well, you look none the worse for it, if you will pardon me saying so!"
>
> He draws himself proudly together and stands at attention. Since his feet are naked I take the click of his heels for granted.
>
> "For seven years I was a soldier of His Majesty the King Emperor!" he exclaims. "Yes Sir, I served with the ranks in

the Indian Army during the Mesopotamian campaign. After the war I was put into the Military Accounts Department because of my superior intelligence!"

I am compelled to smile at his unsolicited testimonial to himself.

"I left the service on account of family trouble, and went through a period of great distress. This induced me to take to the spiritual path and become a *yogi*."

I hand him a card.

"Shall we exchange names?" I suggest.

"My personal name is Subramanya; my caste name is Aiyer," he quickly announces.

"Well, Mr. Subramanya, I am waiting for an explanation of your whispered remark in the house of the Silent Sage."

"And I have been waiting all this time to give it to you! Take your questions to my Master, for he is the wisest man in India, wiser even than the *yogis*."

"So? And have you travelled throughout all India? Have you met all the great *yogis*, that you can make such a statement?"

"I have met several of them, for I know the country from Cape Comorin to Himalayas."

"Well?"

"Sir, I have never met anyone like him, he is a great soul And I want you to meet him."

"Why?"

"Because he has led me to you! It is his power which has drawn you to India!"

This bombastic statement strikes me as being too exaggerated and I begin to recoil from the man. I am always afraid of the rhetorical exaggerations of emotional persons, and it is obvious that the yellow robed *yogi* is highly emotional. His voice, gesture, appearance and atmosphere plainly reveal it.

"I do not understand," is my cold reply.

He falls into further explanations.

"Eight months ago I came into touch with him. For five months I was permitted to stay with him and then I was sent forth on my travels once more. I do not think you are likely to meet with another such man as he. His spiritual gifts are so great that he will answer your unspoken thoughts. You need only be with him a short time to realise his high spiritual degree."

"Are you sure he would welcome my visit?"

"Oh, Sir! Absolutely. It is his guidance which sent me to you."

"Where does he live?"

"On Arunachala — the Hill of the Holy Beacon."

"And where is that?"

"In the North Arcot territory, which lies farther south. I will constitute myself your guide. Let me take you there. My Master will solve your doubts and remove your problems, because he knows the highest truth."

"This sounds quite interesting," I admit reluctantly, "but I regret that the visit is impossible at present. My trunks are packed and I shall be soon leaving for the northeast. There are two important appointments to be fulfilled, you see."

"But this is more important."

"Sorry. We met too late. My arrangements are made and they

cannot be easily altered. I may be back in the South later, but we must leave this journey for the present."

The *yogi* is plainly disappointed.

"You are missing an opportunity, Sir, and .."

I foresee a useless argument, so cut him short.

"I must leave you now. Thanks anyway."

"I refuse to accept" he obstinately declares. "Tomorrow evening I shall call upon you and I hope then to hear that you have changed your mind."

Our conversation abruptly finishes. I watch his strong well-knit yellow robed figure start across the road.

When I reach home, I begin to feel that it is possible I have made an error of judgement. If the Master is worth half the disciple's claims, then he is worth the troublesome journey into the Southern tip of the peninsula. But I have grown somewhat tired of enthusiastic devotees. They sing paeans of praise to their Masters, who prove on investigation to fall lamentably short of the more critical standards of the West. Furthermore sleepless nights and sticky days have rendered my nerves less serene than they should be; thus, the possibility that the journey might prove a wild goose chase looms larger than it should.

Yet argument fails to displace feeling. A queer instinct warns me that there may be some real basis for the *yogi's* ardent insistence on the distinctive claims of his Master. I cannot keep off a sense of self-disappointment. (From *A Search in Secret India*)

Paul Brunton had several notes of introduction to Indian gentlemen, one of which was to Mr. K. S. Venkataramani, the well known author.

Mr. Venkataramani took his European friend to his own Guru 'the Head of South India' (Sri Chandrasekharendra Saraswati, Sankaracharya of Kamakoti Mutt) who was then camping at Chingleput.

The Acharya referred the foreigner to Sri Ramana Maharshi for advice and guidance on matters spiritual. Mr. Brunton returned to his lodging in Madras where Mr. Subramanya was waiting to guide him to Tiruvannamalai. Thus he was brought in contact with his Master. The author records with satisfaction: "It is a singular fact — and perhaps a significant one — that before I can begin to try my luck in this strange quest, fortune herself comes in quest of me."

It is nearly midnight when I returned home...

Out of the darkness, a crouching figure rises and greets me.

"Subramanya!" I exclaim, startled. "What are you doing here?"

The ochre robed *yogi* indulges in one of his tremendous grins.

"Did I not promise to visit you, Sir?" He reminds me reproachfully.

"Of course!"

In the large room, I fire a question at him.

"Your Master, is he called the Maharshi?"

It is now his turn to draw back, astonished.

"How do you know, Sir? Where could you have learnt this?"

"Never mind. Tomorrow we both start for his place. I shall change my plans."

"This is joyful news, Sir."

The events of his stay are recorded in the first chapter of this book. After a short stay there, he left the place, travelled north and had some very interesting experiences. Again destiny came into play and accidentally brought him face to face with the *yogi*, Chandi Das, who advised him to return to Bombay and revisit the master who was awaiting him. Hastily he returned to Bombay and there he was taken ill. So he booked his passage home; nevertheless, pondering over the pros and cons of his revisit to Maharshi, Brunton finally decided to return to him and cancelled his passage home. Just at the time, as if to confirm him in his resolve there came a letter to him (which was following him from place to place) from B. V. Narasimha Swami, the author of *Self-Realisation*[1] who invited him back to Maharshi. Subsequently Mr. Brunton returned to Tiruvannamalai: the later two chapters speak for themselves.

What this book is expected to convey to the reader, may be gathered from the following:

> I journeyed Eastwards in search of the *yogis* and their hermetic knowledge. I can only say that in India I found my faith restored. Not so long ago I was among those who regard God as a hallucination of human fancy, spiritual truth as a mere nebula and providential justice as a confection of infantile idealists. I, too, was somewhat impatient of those who construct theological paradises and who then confidently show you round with an air of being God's estate agents. I had nothing but contempt for what seemed to be the futile, fanatical efforts of uncritical believers.
>
> If, therefore, I have begun to think a little differently about these matters, rest assured that good cause has been given me ....
>
> I did arrive at a new acceptance of the divine. This may seem quite an insignificant and personal thing to do, but as a child

---

[1] Life and Teaching of Sri Ramana Maharshi, pub: Sri Ramanasramam.

of the modern generation which relies on hard facts and cold reason, and which lacks enthusiasm for things religious, I regard it as quite an achievement. This faith was restored in the only way a sceptic would have it restored, not by argument but by the witness of an overwhelming experience. And it was a jungle Sage, an unassuming hermit who had formerly lived for twenty years in a mountain cave, who promoted this vital change in my thinking. It is quite possible that he could not pass a matriculation examination yet I am not ashamed to record in the closing chapters (XVI and XVII) of this book my deep indebtedness to this man. (from *A Search in Secret India*)

The author writes more on this Sage in *The Secret Path* [2] as follows:

Some years ago I wandered for a while through sunbaked Oriental lands, intent on discovering the last remnants of that 'mystic East' about which most of us often hear, but which few of us ever find. During those journeyings I met an unusual man who quickly earned my profound respect and received my humble veneration. For although he belonged by tradition to the class of Wise Men of the East, a class which has largely disappeared from the modern world, he avoided all record of his existence and disdained all efforts to give him publicity.

Time rushes onward like a roaring stream, bearing the human race with it, and drowning our deepest thoughts in its noise. Yet this Sage sat apart, quietly ensconced upon the grassy bank, and watched the gigantic spectacle with a calm Buddha-like smile. The world wants its great men to measure their lives by its puny footrule. But no rule has yet been devised

---

[2] Rider and Co. London.

which will take their full height, for such men, if they are really worth the name, derive their greatness, not from themselves but from another source. And that source stretches far away into the Infinite. Hidden here and there in stray corners of Asia and Africa, a few Seers have preserved the traditions of an ancient wisdom. They live like angels as they guard their treasure. They live outwardly apart, this celestial race, keeping alive the divine secrets, which life and fate have conspired to confide in their care.

The hour of our first meeting is still graven on my memory. I met him unexpectedly. He made no attempt at formal introduction. For an instant, those sibylline eyes gazed into mine, but all the stained earth of my past and the white flowers that had begun to spring upon it, were alike seen during that one tinkle of the bell of time. There in that seated being was a great impersonal force that read the scales of my life with better sight than I could ever hope to do. I had slept in the scented bed of Aphrodite, and he knew it; I had also lured the gnomes of thought to mine for strange enchanted gold in the depths of my spirit; he knew that too. I felt, too, that if I could follow him into his mysterious places of thought, all my miseries would drop away, my resentments turn to toleration, and I would understand life, not merely grumble at it! He interested me much despite the fact that his wisdom was not of a kind which is easily apparent and despite the strong reserve which encircled him. He broke his habitual silence only to answer questions upon such recondite topics as the nature of man's soul, the mystery of God, the strange powers which lie unused in the human mind, and so on, but when he did venture to speak I used to sit enthralled as I listened to his soft voice under burning tropic sun or pale crescent moon. For authority was vested in that calm voice and inspiration gleamed in those luminous eyes. Each phrase that fell from his lips seemed to contain some precious fragment of essential truth. The theologians of a stuffier century taught the doctrine of man's original goodness.

In the presence of this Sage one felt security and inward peace. The spiritual radiations which emanated from him were all-penetrating. I learnt to recognise in his person the sublime truths which he taught, while I was no less hushed into reverence by his incredibly sainted atmosphere. He possessed a deific personality which defies description. I might have taken shorthand notes of the discourses of the Sage. I might even print the record of his speech. But the most important part of his utterances, the subtle and silent flavour of spirituality which emanated from him, can never be reported. If, therefore, I burn literary incense before his bust, it is but a mere fraction of the tribute I ought to pay him.

One could not forget that wonderful pregnant smile of his, with its hint of wisdom and peace won from suffering and experience. He was the most understanding man I have ever known; you could be sure always of some words from him that would smooth your way a little, and that word always *verified* what your deepest feeling told you already.

The words of this Sage still flame out in my memory like beacon lights. 'I pluck golden fruit from rare meetings with wise men,' wrote trans-Atlantic Emerson in his diary, and it is certain that I plucked whole basketfuls during my talks with this man. Our best philosophers of Europe could not hold a candle to him. But the inevitable hour of parting came.

The Hill of the Holy Beacon

AT THE MADRAS TERMINUS OF THE SOUTH Indian Railway, Subramanya and I board a carriage on the Ceylon boat train. For several hours we roll onwards through the most variegated scenes. Green stretches of growing rice alternate with gaunt red hills, shady plantations of stately coconut trees are followed by scattered peasants toiling in the paddy fields.

As I sit at the window, the swift Indian dusk begins to blot out the landscape and I turn my head to muse of other things. I begin to wonder at the strange things which have happened since I have worn the golden ring which Brama has given me. For my plans have changed their face; a concatenation of unexpected circumstances has arisen to drive me farther south, instead of going further east as I have intended. Is it possible, I ask myself, that these golden claws hold a stone which really possesses the mysterious power which the *yogi* has claimed for it? Although I endeavour to keep an open mind, it is difficult for any Westerner of scientifically trained mind to credit the idea. I dismiss the speculation from my mind, but do not succeed in driving away the uncertainty which lurks at the back of my thoughts. Why is it that my footsteps have been so strangely guided to the mountain hermitage whither I am travelling? Why is it that two men, who both wear the yellow robe, have been coupled as destiny's agents to the extent of directing my reluctant eyes towards the Maharshi? I use this word destiny, not in its common sense, but because I am at a loss for a better one. Past experience has taught me full well that seemingly unimportant happenings sometimes play an unexpected part in composing the picture of one's life.

We leave the train, and with it the main line, forty miles from Pondicherry, that pathetic little remnant of France's territorial possessions in India. We go over to a quiet, little used branch railroad which runs into the interior, and wait for nearly two hours in the semi-gloom of a bleak waiting-room. The holy man paces along the bleaker platform outside, his tall figure looking half-ghost, half-real in the starlight. At last the ill-timed train, which puffs infrequently up and down the line, carries us away. There are but few other passengers.

I fall into a fitful, dream-broken sleep which continues for some hours until my companion awakens me. We descend at a little wayside station and the train screeches and grinds away into the silent darkness. Night's life has not quite run out and so we sit in a bare and comfortless little waiting-room, whose small kerosene lamp we light ourselves.

We wait patiently while day fights with darkness for supremacy. When a pale dawn emerges at last, creeping bit by bit through a small barred window in the back of our room, I peer out at such portion of our surroundings as becomes visible. Out of the morning haze there rises the faint outline of a solitary hill apparently some few miles distant. The base is of impressive extent and the body of ample girth, but the head is not to be seen, being yet thick-shrouded in the dawn mists.

My guide ventures outside, where he discovers a man loudly snoring in his tiny bullock cart. A shout or two brings the driver back to this mundane existence thus making him aware of business waiting in the offing. When informed of our destination he seems but too eager to transport us. I gaze somewhat dubiously at his narrow conveyance — a bamboo canopy balanced on two wheels. Anyway, we clamber aboard and the man bundles the luggage after us. The holy man manages to compress himself into the minimum space which a human being can possibly occupy; I crouch under the low canopy with legs dangling out in space; the driver squats upon the shaft between his bulls with his chin almost touching his knees, and the problem of accommodation being thus solved more or less satisfactorily, we bid him be off.

Our progress is anything but rapid, despite the best efforts of a pair of strong, small, white bullocks. These charming creatures are very useful as draught animals in the interior of India, because they endure heat better than horses and are less fastidious in the matter of diet. The customs of the quiet villages and small townships of the interior have not changed very much in the course of centuries. The bullock cart which transported the traveller from place to place in BC 100, transports him still, two thousand years after.

Our driver, whose face is the colour of beaten bronze, has taken much pride in his animals. Their long beautifully curved horns are adorned with shapely gift ornaments; their thin legs have tinkling brass bells tied to them. He guides them by means of a rein threaded through their nostrils. While their feet merrily jog away upon the dust laden road, I watch the quick tropic dawn come on apace.

An attractive landscape shapes itself both on our right and left. No drab flat plain this, for heights and hillocks are not long absent from the eyes whenever one searches the horizon's length. The road traverses a district of red earth dotted with terrains of scrubby thorn-bush and a few bright emerald paddy fields.

A peasant with toil-worn face passes us. No doubt he is going out to his long day's work in the fields. Soon we overtake a girl with a brass water pitcher mounted upon her head. A single vermilion robe is wrapped around her body, but her shoulders are left bare. A blood coloured ruby ornaments one nostril, and a pair of gold bracelets gleam on her arms in the pale morning sunlight. The blackness of her skin reveals her as a Dravidian — as indeed most of the inhabitants of these parts probably are, save the *brahmins* and Muhammadans. These Dravidian girls are usually gay and happy by nature. I find them more talkative than their brown country women and more musical in voice.

The girl stares at us with unfeigned surprise and I guess that Europeans rarely visit this part of the interior.

And so we ride on until the little township is reached. Its houses are prosperous looking and arranged into streets which cluster around three sides of an enormous temple. If I am not mistaken, the latter is a quarter of a mile long. I gather a rough conception of its architectural massiveness a while later when we reach one of its spacious gateways. We halt for a minute or two and I peer inside to register some fleeting glimpses of the place. Its strangeness is as impressive as its size. Never before have I seen a structure like this. A vast quadrangle surrounds the enormous interior, which looks like a labyrinth. I perceive that the four high enclosing walls have been scorched and coloured by hundreds of years of exposure to the fierce tropical sunshine. Each wall is pierced by a single gateway, above which rises a queer superstructure consisting of a giant pagoda. The latter seems strangely like an ornate, sculptured pyramid. Its lower part is built of stone, but the upper portion seems to be thickly plastered brickwork. The pagoda is divided into many storeys, but the entire surface is profusely decorated with a variety of figures and carvings. In addition to these four entrance towers, I count no less than five others which rise up within the interior of the temple. How curiously they remind one of Egyptian pyramids in the similarity of outline!

My last glimpse is of long-roofed cloisters, of serried ranks of flat stone pillars in large numbers, of a great central enclosure, of dim shrines and dark corridors and many little buildings. I make a mental note to explore this interesting place before long.

The bullocks trot off and we emerge into open country again. The scenes which we pass are quite pretty. The road is covered with red dust; on either side there are low bushes and occasional clumps of tall trees. There are many birds hidden among the branches, for I hear the flutter of their wings, as well as the last notes of that beautiful chorus which is their morning song all over the world.

Dotted along the route are a number of charming little wayside shrines. The differences of architectural style surprise me, until I conclude that they have been erected during changing epochs. Some are highly ornate, over-decorated and elaborately carved in the usual Hindu manner, but the larger ones are supported by flat-surfaced pillars which I have seen nowhere else but in the South. There are even two or three shrines whose classical severity of outline is almost Grecian.

I judge that we have now travelled about five or six miles (though we have done only two miles), when we reach the lower slopes of the hill whose vague outline I had seen from the station. It rises like a reddish brown giant in the clear morning sunlight. The mists have now rolled away, revealing a broad skyline at the top. It is an isolated upland of red soil and brown rock, barren for the most part, with large tracts almost treeless, and with masses of stone split into great boulders tossed about in chaotic disorder.

"Arunachala! The sacred red mountain!" exclaims my companion, noticing the direction of my gaze. A fervent expression of adoration passes across his face. He is momentarily rapt in ecstasy like some medieval saint.

I ask him, "Does the name mean anything?"

"I have just given you the meaning," he replies with a smile. "The name is composed of two words 'Aruna' and 'Achala', which means red mountain and since it is also the name of the presiding deity of the temple, its full translation should be 'sacred red mountain'."

"Then where does the holy beacon come in?"

"Ah! Once a year the temple priests celebrate their central festival. Immediately that occurs within the temple, a huge fire blazes out on top of the mountain, its flame being fed with vast quantities of melted butter (ghee) and camphor. It burns for many days and can be seen for many miles around. Whoever sees it, at once prostrates himself before it. It symbolises the fact that this mountain is sacred ground, overshadowed by a great deity."

The hill now towers over our heads. It is not without its rugged grandeur, this lonely peak patterned with red, brown and grey boulders, thrusting its flat head thousands of feet into the pearly sky. Whether the holy man's words have affected me or whether for some unaccountable cause, I find a queer feeling of awe arising in me as I meditate upon the picture of the sacred mountain, as I gaze up wonderingly at the steep incline of Arunachala.

"Do you know," whispers my companion, "that this mountain is not only esteemed holy ground, but the local traditions dare to assert that the gods placed it there to mark the spiritual centre of the world!"

This little bit of legend forces me to smile. How naive it is!

At length I learn that we are approaching the Maharshi's hermitage. We turn aside from the road and move down a rough path which brings us to a thick grove of coconut and mango trees. We cross this until the path suddenly comes to an abrupt termination before an unlocked gate. The driver descends, pushes the gate open, and then drives us into a large unpaved courtyard.

I stretch out my cramped limbs, descend to the ground, and look around.

The cloistered domain of the Maharshi is hemmed in at the front by closely growing trees and a thickly clustered garden; it is screened at the back and side by hedgerows of shrub and cactus, while away to the west stretches the scrub jungle and what appears to be dense forest. It is most picturesquely placed on a lower spur of the hill. Secluded and apart, it seems a fitting spot for those who wish to pursue profound themes of meditation.

Two small buildings with thatched roofs occupy the left side of the courtyard. Adjoining them stands a long, modern structure, whose red-tiled roof comes sharply down into overhanging eaves. A small verandah stretches across a part of the front.

The centre of the courtyard is marked by a large well. I watch a boy, who is naked to the waist and dark-skinned to the point of blackness, slowly draw a bucket of water to the surface with the aid of a creaking hand windlass.

The sound of our entry brings a few men out of the buildings into the courtyard. Their dress is extremely varied. One is garbed in nothing but a ragged loin-cloth, but another is prosperously attired in a white silk robe. They stare questioningly at us. My guide grins hugely, evidently enjoying their astonishment. He crosses to them and says something in Tamil. The expression on their faces changes immediately, for they smile in unison and beam at me with pleasure. I like their faces and their bearing.

"We shall now go into the hall of the Maharshi," announces the holy man of the yellow robe, bidding me follow him. I pause outside the uncovered stone verandah and remove my shoes. I gather up the little pile of fruits which I have brought as an offering, and pass into an open doorway.

Twenty faces flash their eyes upon us. Their owners are squatting in half-circles on a dark grey floor paved with Cuddapah slabs. They are grouped at a respectful distance from the corner which lies farthest to the right hand of the door. Apparently everyone has been facing this corner just prior to our entry. I glance there for a moment and perceive a seated figure upon a long white divan, but it suffices to tell me that here indeed is the Maharshi.

My guide approaches the divan, prostrates himself prone on the floor, and buries his eyes under folded hands.

The divan is but a few paces away from a broad high window in the end wall. The light falls clearly upon the Maharshi and I can take in every detail of his profile, for he is seated gazing rigidly through the window in the precise direction whence we have come this morning. His head does not move, so, thinking to catch his eye and greet him as I offer the fruits, I move quietly over to the window, place the gift before him, and retreat a pace or two.

A small iron brazier stands before his couch. It is filled with burning charcoal, and a pleasant odour tells me that some aromatic powder has been thrown on the glowing embers. Close by is an incense burner filled with joss sticks. Threads of bluish grey smoke arise and float in the air, but the pungent perfume is quite different.

I fold a thin cotton blanket upon the floor and sit down, gazing expectantly at the silent figure in such a rigid attitude upon the couch. The Maharshi's body is almost nude, except for a thin, narrow loin cloth, but that is common enough in these parts. His skin is slightly copper coloured, yet quite fair in comparison with that of the average South Indian. I judge him to be a tall man; his age is somewhere in the early fifties. His head, which is covered with closely cropped grey hair, is well formed. The high and broad expanse of forehead gives intellectual distinction to his personality. His features are more European than Indian. Such is my first impression.

The couch is covered with white cushions and the Maharshi's feet rest upon a magnificently marked tiger skin.

Pin-drop silence prevails throughout the long hall. The Sage remains perfectly still, motionless, quite undisturbed at our arrival. A swarthy disciple sits on the floor at the other side of the divan. He breaks into the quietude by beginning to pull at a rope which works a *punkah* fan made of plaited khaki. The fan is fixed to a wooden beam and suspended immediately above the Sage's head. I listen to its rhythmic purring, the while I look full into the eyes of the seated figure in the hope of catching his notice. They are dark brown, medium sized and wide open.

If he is aware of my presence, he betrays no hint, gives no sign. His body is supernaturally quiet, as steady as a statue. Not once does he catch my gaze for his eyes continue to look into remote space, and infinitely remote it seems. I find this scene strangely reminiscent. Where have I seen its like? I rummage through the portrait gallery of memory and find the picture of the Sage Who Never Speaks, that recluse whom I visited in his isolated cottage near Madras, that man whose body seemed cut from stone, so motionless it was. There is a curious similarity in this unfamiliar stillness of body which I now behold in the Maharshi.

It is an ancient theory of mine that one can take the inventory of a man's soul from his eyes. But before those of the Maharshi I hesitate, puzzled and baffled.

The minutes creep by with unutterable slowness. First they mount up to a half-hour by the hermitage clock which hangs on a wall; this too passes by and becomes a whole hour. Yet no one dares to speak. I reach a point of visual concentration where I have forgotten the existence of all save this silent figure on the couch. My offering of fruit remains unregarded on the small carved table which stands before him.

My guide has given me no warning that his Master will receive me as I had been received by the Sage Who Never Speaks. It has come upon me abruptly, this strange reception characterised by complete indifference. The first thought which would come into the mind of any European, "Is this man merely posing for the benefit of his devotees?" crosses my mind once or twice, but I soon rule it out. He is certainly in a trance condition, though my guide has not informed me that his Master indulges in trances. The next thought which occupies my mind, "Is this state of mystical contemplation nothing more than meaningless vacancy?" has a longer sway, but I let it go for the simple reason that I cannot answer it.

There is something in this man which holds my attention as steel filings are held by a magnet. I cannot turn my gaze away from him. My initial bewilderment, my perplexity at being totally ignored, slowly fade away as this strange fascination begins to grip me more firmly. But it is not till the second hour of the uncommon scene that I become aware of a silent, resistless change which is taking place within my mind. One by one, the questions which I prepared in the train with such meticulous accuracy drop away. For it does not now seem to matter whether they are asked or not, and it does not matter whether I solve the problems which have hitherto troubled me. I know only that a steady river of quietness seems to be flowing near me; that a great peace is penetrating the inner reaches of my being, and that my thought-tortured brain is beginning to arrive at some rest.

How small seem those questions which I have asked myself with such frequency? How petty grows the panorama of the last years! I perceive with sudden clarity that intellect creates its own problems and then makes itself miserable trying to solve them. This is indeed a novel concept to enter the mind of one who has hitherto placed such high value upon intellect.

I surrender myself to the steadily deepening sense of restfulness until two hours have passed. The passage of time now provokes no irritation, because I feel that the chains of mind-made problems are being broken and thrown away. And then, little by little, a new question takes the field of consciousness.

"Does this man, the Maharshi, emanate the perfume of spiritual peace as the flower emanates fragrance from its petals?"

I do not consider myself a competent person to apprehend spirituality, but I have personal reactions to other people. The dawning suspicion that the mysterious peace which has arisen within me must be attributed to the geographical situation in which I am now placed, is my reaction to the personality of the Maharshi. I begin to wonder whether, by some radioactivity of the soul, some unknown telepathic process, the stillness which invades the troubled waters of my own soul really comes from him. Yet he remains completely impassive completely unaware of my very existence, it seems.

Comes the first ripple. Someone approaches me and whispers in my ear. "Did you not wish to question the Maharshi?"

He may have lost patience, this quondam guide of mine. More likely, he imagines that I, a restless European, have reached the limit of my own patience. Alas, my inquisitive friend! Truly I came here to question your Master, but now ... I, who am at peace with all the world and with myself, why should I trouble my head with questions? I feel that the ship of my soul is beginning to slip its moorings; a wonderful sea waits to be crossed; yet you would draw me back to the noisy port of this world, just when I am about to start the great adventure!

But the spell is broken. As if this infelicitous intrusion is a signal, figures rise from the floor and begin to move about the hall, voices float up to my hearing, and wonder of wonders! — the dark brown eyes of the Maharshi flicker once or twice. Then the head turns, the face moves slowly, very slowly, and bends downward at an angle. A few more moments and it has brought me into the ambit of its vision. For the first time the Sage's mysterious gaze is directed upon me. It is plain that he has now awakened from his long trance.

The intruder, thinking perhaps that my lack of response is a sign that I have not heard him, repeats his question aloud. But in those lustrous eyes which are gently staring at me, I read another question, albeit unspoken:

"Can it be — is it possible — that you are still tormented with distracting doubts when you have now glimpsed the deep mental peace which you — and all men — may attain?"

The peace overwhelms me. I turn to the guide and answer:

"No. There is nothing I care to ask now. Another time......"

I feel now that some explanation of my visit is required of me, not by the Maharshi himself but by the little crowd which has begun to talk so animatedly. I know from the accounts of my guide that only a handful of these people are resident disciples, and that the others are visitors from the country around. Strangely enough, at this point my guide himself arises and makes the required introduction. He speaks energetically in Tamil, using a wealth of gesture while he explains matters to the assembled company. I fear that the explanation is mixing a little fable with his facts, for it draws cries of wonder.

The midday meal is over. The sun unmercifully raises the afternoon temperature to a degree I have never before experienced. But then, we are now in a latitude not so far from the Equator. For once I am grateful that India is favoured with a climate which does not foster activity, because most of the people have disappeared into the shady groves to take a siesta. I can, therefore, approach the Maharshi in the way I prefer, without undue notice or fuss.

I enter the large hall and sit down near him. He half reclines upon some white cushions placed on the divan. An attendant pulls steadily at the cord which operates the *punkah* fan. The soft burr of the rope and the gentle swish of the fan as it moves through the sultry air sound pleasantly in my ears.

The Maharshi holds a folded manuscript book in his hands; he is writing something with extreme slowness. A few minutes after my entry he puts the book aside and calls a disciple. A few words pass between them in Tamil and the man tells me that his Master wishes to reiterate his regrets at my inability to partake of their food. He explains that they live a simple life and never having catered for Europeans before do not know what the latter eat. I thank the Maharshi, and say that I shall be glad to share their unspiced dishes with them; for the rest, I shall procure some food from the township. I add that I regard the question of diet as being far less important than the quest which has brought me to his hermitage.

The Sage listens intently, his face calm, imperturbable and non-committal.

"It is a good object," he comments at length.

This encourages me to enlarge upon the same theme.

"Master, I have studied our Western philosophies and sciences, lived and worked among the people of our crowded cities, tasted their pleasures and allowed myself to be caught up into their ambitions. Yet I have also gone into solitary places and wandered there amid the loneliness of deep thought. I have questioned the sages of the West; now I have turned my face towards the East. I seek more light."

The Maharshi nods his head, as if to say, "Yes, I quite understand."

"I have heard many opinions, listened to many theories. Intellectual proofs of one belief or another lie piled up all around me. I am tired of them, sceptical of anything which cannot be proved by personal experience. Forgive me for saying so, but I am not religious. Is there anything beyond man's material existence? If so, how can I realize it for myself?"

The three or four devotees who are gathered around us stare in surprise. Have I offended the subtle etiquette of the hermitage by speaking so brusquely and boldly to their Master? I do not know; perhaps I do not care. The accumulated weight of many years' desire has unexpectedly escaped my control and passed beyond my lips. If the Maharshi is the right kind of man, surely he will understand and brush aside mere lapses from convention.

He makes no verbal reply but appears to have dropped into some train of thought. Because there is nothing else to do and because my tongue has now been loosened, I address him for the third time:

"The wise men of the West, our scientists, are greatly honoured for their cleverness. Yet they have confessed that they can throw but little light upon the hidden truth behind life. It is said that there are some in your land who can give what our Western sages fail to reveal. Is this so? Can you assist me to experience enlightenment? Or is the search itself a mere delusion?"

I have now reached my conversational objective and decide to await the Maharshi's response. He continues to stare thoughtfully at me. Perhaps he is pondering over my questions. Ten minutes pass in silence.

At last his lips open and he says gently:

"You say I. '*I* want to know.' Tell me, who is that *I*?"

What does he mean? He has now cut across the services of the interpreter and speaks direct to me in English. Bewilderment creeps across my brain.

"I am afraid I do not understand your question," I reply blankly.

"Is it not clear? Think again!"

I puzzle over his words once more. An idea suddenly flashes into my head. I point a finger towards myself and mention my name.

"And do you know him?"

"All my life!" I smile back at him.

"But that is only your body! Again I ask, 'Who are *you*'?"

I cannot find a ready answer to this extraordinary query.

The Maharshi continues:

"Know first that *I* and then you shall know the truth."

My mind hazes again. I am deeply puzzled. This bewilderment finds verbal expression. But the Maharshi has evidently reached the limit of his English, for he turns to the interpreter and the answer is slowly translated to me:

"There is only one thing to be done. Look into your own self. Do this in the right way and you shall find the answer to all your problems."

It is a strange rejoinder. But I ask him:

"What must one do? What method can I pursue?"

"Through deep reflection on the nature of one's self and through constant meditation, the light can be found."

"I have frequently given myself up to meditation upon the truth, but I see no signs of progress."

"How do you know that no progress has been made? It is not easy to perceive one's progress in the spiritual realm."

"Is help of a Master necessary?"

"It might be."

"Can a Master help a man to look into his own self in the way you suggest?"

"He can give the man all that he needs for this quest. Such a thing can be perceived through personal experience."

"How long will it take to get some enlightenment with a Master's help?"

"It all depends on the maturity of the seeker's mind. The gunpowder catches fire in an instant, while much time is needed to set fire to the coal."

I receive a queer feeling that the Sage dislikes to discuss the subject of Masters and their methods. Yet my mental pertinacity is strong enough to override this feeling, and I address a further question on the matter to him. He turns a stolid face toward the window, gazes out at the expanse of hilly landscape beyond, and vouchsafes no answer. I take the hint and drop the subject.

"Will the Maharshi express an opinion about the future of the world, for we are living in critical times?"

"Why should you trouble yourself about the future?" demands the Sage. "You do not even properly know about the present! Take care of the present; the future will then take care of itself."

Another rebuff! But I do not yield so easily on this occasion, for I come from a world where the tragedies of life press far more heavily on people than they do in this peaceful jungle retreat.

"Will the world soon enter a new era of friendliness and mutual help, or will it go down into chaos and war?" I persist.

The Maharshi does not seem at all pleased, but nevertheless he makes a reply.

"There is One who governs the world, and it is His lookout to look after the world. He who has given life to the world knows how to look after it also. He bears the burden of this world, not you."

"Yet if one looks around with unprejudiced eyes, it is difficult to see where this benevolent regard comes in," I object.

The Sage appears to be still less pleased. Yet his answer comes:

"As you are, so is the world. Without understanding yourself, what is the use of trying to understand the world? This is a question that seekers after truth need not consider. People waste their energies over all such questions. First, find out the truth behind yourself; then you will be in a better position to understand the truth behind the world, of which yourself is a part."

There is an abrupt pause. An attendant approaches and lights another incense stick. The Maharshi watches the blue smoke curl its way upwards and then picks up his manuscript book. He unfolds its pages and begins to work on it again, thus dismissing me from the field of his attention.

This renewed indifference of his plays like cold water upon my self-esteem. I sit around for another quarter of an hour, but I can see that he is in no mood to answer my questions. Feeling that our conversation is really at an end, I rise from the tiled floor, place my hands together in farewell, and leave him.

§

I have sent someone to the township with orders to fetch a conveyance, for I wish to inspect the temple. I request him to find a horsed carriage, if there is one in the place, for a bullock cart is picturesque to look at, but hardly as rapid and comfortable as one could wish.

I find a two-wheeled pony carriage waiting for me as I enter the courtyard. It possesses no seat, but such an item no longer troubles me. The driver is a fierce looking fellow with a soiled red turban on his head. His only other garment is a long piece of unbleached cloth made into a waistband with one end passing between his thighs and then tucking into his waist.

A long, dusty ride, and then at last the entrance to the great temple, with its rising storeys of carved reliefs, greets us. I leave the carriage and begin a cursory exploration.

"I cannot say how old is the temple of Arunachala," remarks my companion in response to a question, "but as you can see its age must extend back hundreds of years."

Around the gates and in the approaches to the temple are a few little shops and gaudy booths, set up under overhanging palms. Beside them sit humbly dressed vendors of holy pictures and sellers of little brass images of Siva and other gods. I am struck by the preponderance of representations of the former deity, for in other places Krishna and Rama seem to hold first place. My guide offers an explanation.

"According to our sacred legends, God Siva once appeared as a flame of fire on the top of the sacred red mountain. Therefore, the priests of the temple light the large beacon once a year in memory of this event which must have happened thousands of years ago. I suppose the temple was built to celebrate it, as Siva still overshadows the mountain."

A few pilgrims are idly examining the stalls where one can buy not only these little brass deities, but also gaudy chromolithographs picturing some event from the sacred stories, books of a religious character, blotchily printed in Tamil and Telugu languages, and coloured paints wherewith to mark on one's forehead the fitting caste or sect symbol.

A leprous beggar comes hesitatingly towards me. The flesh of his limbs is crumbling away. He is apparently not certain whether I shall have him driven off, poor fellow, or whether he will be able to touch my pity. His face is rigid with his terrible disease. I feel ashamed as I place some alms on the ground, but I fear to touch him.

The gateway, which is shaped into a pyramid of carven figures, next engages my attention. This great towered portico looks like some pyramid out of Egypt with its pointed top chopped off. Together with its three fellows, it dominates the countryside. One sees them miles away long before one approaches them.

The face of the pagodas is lined with profuse carvings and quaint little statues. The subjects have been drawn from sacred myth and legend. They represent a queer jumble. One perceives the solitary forms of Hindu divinities entranced into devout meditation, or observes their intertwined shapes engaged in amorous embraces, and one wonders. It reminds one that there is something in Hinduism for all tastes, such is the all-inclusive nature of this creed.

I enter the precincts of the temple, to find myself in part of an enormous quadrangle. The vast structure encloses a labyrinth of colonnades, cloisters, galleries, shrines, rooms, covered and uncovered spaces. Here is no stone building whose columned beauty stays one's emotions in a few minutes of silent wonder, as do those courts of the deities near Athens, but rather a gloomy sanctuary of dark mysteries. The vast recesses awe me with their chill air of aloofness. The place is a maze, but my companion walks with confident feet. Outside, the pagodas have looked attractive with their reddish stone colouring, but inside the stonework is granite grey.

We pass through a long cloister with solid walls and flat, quaintly carved pillars supporting the roofs. We move into dim corridors and dark chambers and eventually arrive at a vast portico which stands in the outer court of this ancient fane.

"The Hall of a Thousand Pillars!" announces my guide as I gaze at the time-greyed structure. A serried row of flat, carved, gigantic stone columns stretches before me. The place is lonely and deserted; its monstrous pillars loom mysteriously out of the semi-gloom. I approach them more closely to study the old carvings which line many of their faces. Each pillar is composed of a single block of stone, and even the roof which it supports is composed of large pieces of flat stone. Once again I see gods and goddesses disporting themselves with the help of the sculptor's art; once again the carved faces of animals familiar and unfamiliar stare at me.

We wander on across the flagstones of these pillared galleries, pass through dark passages lit here and there by small bowl lamps, whose wicks are sunk in castor oil, and thus arrive near a central enclosure. It is pleasant to emerge once again in the bright sunshine as we cross over to the enclosure. One can now observe the five shorter pagodas which dot the interior of the temple.

They are formed precisely like the pyramidal towers which mark the entrance gateways in the high-walled quadrangle. I examine the one which stands near us and arrive at the conclusion that it is built of brick, and that its decorated surface is not really stone-carved, but modelled out of baked clay or some durable plaster. Some of the figures have evidently been picked out with paint, but the colours have now faded.

We enter the enclosure and after wandering through some more long, dark passages in this stupendous temple, my guide warns me that we are approaching the central shrine, where European feet may not walk. But though the holy of holies is forbidden to the infidel, yet the latter is allowed to catch a glimpse from a dark corridor which leads to the threshold. As if to confirm his warning I hear the beating of drums, the banging of gongs and the droning incantations of priests mingling into a monotonous rhythm that sounds rather eerie in the darkness of the old sanctuary.

I take my glimpse, expectantly. Out of the gloom there rises a golden flame set before an idol, two or three dim altar lights, and the sight of a few worshippers engaged in some ritual. I cannot distinguish the forms of the priests and the musicians, but now I hear the conch, horn and the cymbal add their harsh, weird notes to the music.

My companion whispers that it would be better for me not to stay any longer, as my presence will be decidedly unwelcome to the priests. Thereupon we withdraw into the somnolent sanctity of the outer parts of the temple. My exploration is at an end.

When we reach the gateway once more, I have to step aside because an elderly *brahmin* sits on the ground in the middle of the path with a little brass water-jug beside him. He paints a gaudy caste mark on his forehead, holding a broken bit of mirror in his left hand. The red and white trident which presently appears upon his brow — sign of an orthodox Hindu of the South — gives him, in Western eyes, the grotesque appearance of a clown. A shrivelled old man, who sits in a booth by the temple gates and sells little images of holy Siva, raises his eyes to meet mine and I pause to buy something at his unuttered request.

Somewhere in the far end of the township I espy the gleaming whiteness of a couple of minarets. So I leave the temple and drive to the local mosque. Something inside me always thrills to the graceful arches of a mosque and to the delicate beauty of cupolas. Once again I remove my shoes and enter the charming white building. How well it has been planned, for its vaulted height inevitably elevates one's mood! There are a few worshippers present; they sit, kneel or prostrate themselves upon their small, colourful prayer rugs. There are no mysterious shrines here, no gaudy images, for the Prophet has written that nothing shall come between a man and God, not even a priest! All worshippers are equal before the face of Allah. There is neither priest nor pundit, no hierarchy of superior beings to interpose themselves in a man's thoughts when he turns towards Mecca.

As we return through the main street I note the money-changers' booths, the sweetmeat stalls, the cloth merchants' shops and the sellers of grain and rice — all existing for the benefit of pilgrims to the ancient sanctuary which has called the place into being.

I am now eager to get back to the Maharshi and the driver urges his pony to cover the distance which lies before us at a rapid pace. I turn my head and take a final glimpse of the temple of Arunachala. The nine sculptured towers rise like pylons into the air. They speak to me of the patient toil in the name of God which has gone into the making of the old temple, for it has undoubtedly taken more than a man's lifetime to construct. And again that queer reminiscence of Egypt penetrates my mind.

Even the domestic architecture of the streets possesses an Egyptian character in the low houses and thick walls.

Shall a day ever come when these temples will be abandoned and left, silent and deserted, to crumble slowly into the red and grey dust whence they have emerged? Or will man find new gods and build new fanes wherein to worship them?

While our pony gallops along the road towards the hermitage which lies on one of the slopes of yonder rock strewn hill, I realise with a catch in my breath that Nature is unrolling an entire pageant of beauty back before our eyes. How often have I waited for this hour in the East, when the sun, with much splendour, goes to rest upon its bed of night! An Oriental sunset holds the heart with its lovely play of vivid colours. And yet the whole event is over so quickly, an affair of less than half an hour.

Those lingering autumnal evenings of Europe are almost unknown here. Out in the west a great flaming ball of fire begins its visible descent into the jungle. It assumes the most striking orange hue as a prelude to its rapid disappearance from the vault of heaven. The sky around it takes on all the colours of the spectrum, providing our eyes with an artistic feast which no painter could ever provide. The field and groves around us have entered into an entranced stillness. No more can the chirruping of little birds be heard. The giant circle of red fire is quickly fading into some other dimension. Evening's curtain falls thicker yet and soon the whole panorama of thrusting tongues of flame and outspread colours sinks away into darkness.

The calmness sinks into my thoughts, the loveliness of it all touches my heart. How can one forget these benign minutes which the fates have portioned us, when they make us play with the thought that, under the cruel face of life, a benevolent and beautiful Power may yet be hiding? These minutes put our commonplace hours to shame. Out of the dark void they come like meteors, to light a transient trail of hope and then to pass away from our ken.

§

Fireflies whirl about the hermitage garden, drawing strange patterns of light on the background of darkness, as we drive in the palm-fringed courtyard. And when I enter the long hall and drop to a seat on the floor, the sublime silence appears to have reached this place and pervaded the air.

The assembled company squats in rows around the hall, but among them there is no noise and no talk. Upon the corner couch sits the Maharshi, his feet folded beneath him, his hands resting unconcernedly upon his knees. His figure strikes me anew as being simple, modest; yet withal it is dignified and impressive. His head is nobly poised, like the head of some Homeric sage. His eyes gaze immovably towards the far end of the hall. That strange steadiness of sight is as puzzling as ever. Has he been merely watching through the window the last ray of light fade out of the sky, or is he so wrapt in some dreamlike abstraction as to see naught of this material world at all?

The usual cloud of incense floats among the rafters of the roof. I settle down and try to fix my eyes on the Maharshi, but after a while feel a delicate urge to close them. It is not long before I fall into a half sleep lulled by the intangible peace which, in the Sage's proximity, begins to penetrate me more deeply. Ultimately there comes a gap in my consciousness and then I experience a vivid dream.

It seems that I become a little boy of five. I stand on a rough path which winds up and around the sacred hill of Arunachala, and hold the Maharshi's hand; but now he is a great towering figure at my side, for he seems to have grown to giant's size. He leads me away from the hermitage and, despite the impenetrable darkness of the night guides me along the path which we both slowly walk together. After a while the stars and the moon conspire to bestow a faint light upon our surroundings. I notice that the Maharshi carefully guides me around fissures in the rocky soil and between monstrous boulders that are shakily perched. The hill is steep and our ascent is slow. Hidden in narrow clefts between the rocks and boulders or sheltered by clusters of low bushes, tiny hermitages and inhabited caves come into view. As we pass by, the inhabitants emerge to greet us and, although their forms take on a ghostly appearance in the starlight, I recognise that they are *yogis* of varying kinds. We never stop for them, but continue to walk until the top of the peak is reached. We halt at last, my heart throbbing with a strange anticipation of some momentous event about to befall me.

The Maharshi turns and looks down into my face; I, in turn, gaze expectantly up at him. I become aware of a mysterious change taking place with great rapidity in my heart and mind. The old motives which have lured me on begin to desert me. The urgent desires which have sent my feet hither and thither vanish with incredible swiftness. The dislikes, misunderstandings, coldnesses and selfishness which have marked my dealings with many of my fellows collapse into the abyss of nothingness. An untellable peace falls upon me and I know that there is nothing further that I shall ask from life.

Suddenly the Maharshi bids me turn my gaze away to the bottom of the hill. I obediently do so and to my astonishment discover that the Western hemisphere of our globe lies stretched out far below. It is crowded with millions of people; I can vaguely discern them as masses of forms, but the night's darkness still enshrouds them.

The Sage's voice comes to my ears, his words slowly uttered:

"When you go back there, you shall have this peace which you now feel, but its price will be that you shall henceforth cast aside the idea that you are this body or this brain. When this peace will flow into you, then you shall have to forget your own self, for you will have turned your life over to THAT!"

And the Maharshi places one end of a thread of silver light in my hand.

I awaken from that extraordinarily vivid dream with the sense of its penetrating sublimity yet upon me. Immediately the Maharshi's eyes meet mine. His face is now turned in my direction, and he is looking fixedly into my eyes.

What lies behind that dream? For the desires and bitternesses of personal life fade for a while into oblivion. That condition of lofty indifference to self and profound pity for my fellows which I have dreamt into being, does not take its departure even though I am now awake. It is a strange experience.

But if the dream has any verity in it, then the thing will not last; it is not yet for me.

How long have I been sunk in dream? For everyone in the hall now begins to rise and to prepare for sleep. I must perforce follow the example.

It is too stuffy to sleep in that long, sparsely ventilated hall, so I choose the courtyard. A tall, grey-bearded disciple brings me a lantern and advises me to keep it burning throughout the night. There is a possibility of unwelcome visitors, such as snakes and even cheetahs, but they are likely to keep clear of a light.

The earth is baked hard and I possess no mattress, with the result that I do not fall asleep for some hours. But no matter — I have enough to think over, for I feel that in the Maharshi I have met the most mysterious personality whom life has yet brought within the orbit of my experience.

The Sage seems to carry something of great moment to me, yet I cannot easily determine its precise nature. It is intangible, imponderable, perhaps spiritual. Each time I think of him tonight, each time I remember that vivid dream, a peculiar sensation pierces me and causes my heart to throb with vague, but lofty expectations.

§

During the ensuing days I endeavour to get into closer contact with the Maharshi, but fail. There are three reasons for this failure. The first arises naturally out of his own reserved nature, his obvious dislike of argument and discussion, his stolid indifference to one's beliefs and opinions. It becomes perfectly obvious that the Sage has no wish to convert anyone to his own ideas, whatever they may be, and no desire to add a single person to his following.

The second cause is certainly a strange one, but nevertheless exists. Since the evening of that peculiar dream, I feel a great awe whenever I enter his presence. The questions which would otherwise have come chatteringly from my lips are hushed, because it seems almost sacrilege to regard him as a person with whom one can talk and argue on an equal plane, so far as common humanity is concerned.

The third cause of my failure is simple enough. Almost always there are several other persons present in the hall, and I feel disinclined to bring out my private thoughts in their presence. After all, I am a stranger to them and a foreigner in this district. That I voice a different language to some of them is a fact of little import, but that I possess a cynical, sceptical outlook unstirred by religious emotion is a fact of much import when I attempt to give utterance to that outlook. I have no desire to hurt their pious susceptibilities, but I have also no desire to discuss matters from an angle which makes little appeal to me. So, to some extent, this thing makes me tongue-tied.

It is not easy to find a smooth way across all three barriers; several times I am on the point of putting a question to the Maharshi, but one of the three factors intervenes to cause my failure.

My proposed weekend quickly passes and I extend it to a week. The first conversation which I have had with the Maharshi worthy of the name is likewise the last. Beyond one or two quite perfunctory and conventional scraps of talk, I find myself unable to get to grips with the man.

The week passes and I extend it to a fortnight. Each day I sense the beautiful peace of the Sage's mental atmosphere, the serenity which pervades the very air around him.

The last day of my visit arrives and yet I am no closer to him. My stay has been a tantalising mixture of sublime moods and disappointing failures to effect any worthwhile personal contact with the Maharshi. I look around the hall and feel a slight despondency. Most of these men speak a different language, both outwardly and inwardly; how can I hope to come closer to them? I look at the Sage himself. He sits there on Olympian heights and watches the panorama of life as one apart. There is a mysterious property in this man which differentiates him from all others I have met. I feel, somehow, that he does not belong to us, the human race, so much as he belongs to Nature, to the solitary peak which rises abruptly behind the hermitage, to the rough tract of jungle which stretches away into distant forests, and to the impenetrable sky which fills all space.

Something of the stony, motionless quality of lonely Arunachala seems to have entered into the Maharshi. I have learnt that he has lived on the hill for about twenty years and refuses to leave it, even for a single short journey. Such a close association must inevitably have its effects on a man's character. I know that he loves this hill, for someone has translated a few lines of a charming but pathetic poem which the Sage has written to express this love. Just as this isolated hill rises out of the jungle's edge and rears its squat head to the sky, so does this strange man raise his own head in solitary grandeur, nay, in uniqueness, out of the jungle of common humanity. Just as Arunachala, Hill of the Sacred Beacon, stands aloof, apart from the irregular chain of hills which girdles the entire landscape, so does the Maharshi remain mysteriously aloof even when surrounded by his own devotees, men who have loved him and lived near him for years. The impersonal, impenetrable quality of all Nature — so peculiarly exemplified in this sacred mountain — has somehow entered into him. It has segregated him from his weak fellows, perhaps forever. Sometimes I catch myself wishing that he would be a little more human, a little more susceptible to what seems so normal to us, but so like feeble failings when exhibited in his impersonal presence. And yet, if he has really attained to some sublime realisation beyond the common, how can one expect him to do so without leaving his laggard race behind forever? Why is it that under his strange glance I invariably experience a peculiar expectancy, as though some stupendous revelation will soon be made to me?

Yet beyond the moods of palpable serenity and the dream which stars itself in the sky of memory, no verbal or other revelation has been communicated to me. I feel somewhat desperate at the pressure of time. Almost a fortnight gone and only a single talk that means anything! Even the abruptness in the Sage's voice has helped, metaphorically, to keep me off. This unwanted reception is also unexpected, for I have not forgotten the glowing inducements to come here with which the yellow-robed holy man plied me. The tantalising thing is that I want the Sage, above all other men, to loosen his tongue for me, because a single thought has somehow taken possession of my mind. I do not obtain it by any process of ratiocination; it comes unbidden, entirely of its own accord.

"This man has freed himself from all problems, and no woe can touch him."

Such is the purport of this dominating thought.

I resolve to make a fresh attempt to force my questions into voice and to engage the Maharshi in answer to them. I go out to one of his old disciples, who is doing some work in the adjoining cottage and who has been exceedingly kind to me, and tell him earnestly of my wish to have a final chat with his Master. I confess that I feel too shy to tackle the Sage myself. The disciple smiles compassionately. He leaves me and soon returns with the news that his Master will be very pleased to grant the interview.

I hasten back to the hall and sit down conveniently near the divan. The Maharshi turns his face immediately, his mouth relaxing into a pleasant greeting. Straightaway, I feel at ease and begin to question him.

"The *yogis* say that one must renounce this world and go off into secluded jungles or mountains, if one wishes to find truth. Such things can hardly be done in the West; our lives are so different. Do you agree with the *yogis*?"

The Maharshi turns to a *brahmin* disciple of courtly countenance. The latter translates his answer to me:

"The life of action need not be renounced. If you will meditate for an hour or two every day, you can then carry on with your duties. If you meditate in the right manner, then the current of mind induced will continue to flow even in the midst of your work. It is as though there were two ways of expressing the same idea; the same line which you take in meditation will be expressed in your activities."

"What will be the result of doing that?"

"As you go on you will find that your attitude towards people, events and objects will gradually change. Your actions will tend to follow your meditations of their own accord."

"Then you do not agree with the *yogis*?" I try to pin him down.

But the Maharshi eludes a direct answer.

"A man should surrender the personal selfishness which binds him to this world. Giving up the false self is the true renunciation."

"How is it possible to become selfless while leading a life of worldly activity?"

"There is no conflict between work and wisdom."

"Do you mean that one can continue all the old activities in one's profession, for instance, and at the same time get enlightenment?"

"Why not? But in that case one will not think that it is the old personality which is doing the work, because one's consciousness will gradually become transferred until it is centred in That which is beyond the little self."

"If a person is engaged in work, there will be little time left for him to meditate."

The Maharshi seems quite unperturbed at my poser.

"Setting apart time for meditation is only for the merest spiritual novices," he replies. "A man who is advancing will begin to enjoy the deeper beatitude, whether he is at work or not. While his hands are in society, he keeps his head cool in solitude."

"Then you do not teach the way of *yoga*?"

"The *yogi* tries to drive his mind to the goal, as a cowherd drives a bull with a stick, but on this path the seeker coaxes the bull by holding out a handful of grass."

"How is that done?"

"You have to ask yourself the question, 'Who am I?'. This investigation will lead in the end to the discovery of something within you which is behind the mind. Solve that great problem, and you will solve all other problems thereby."

There is a pause as I try to digest his answer. From the square-framed and barred hole in the wall which does duty as a window, as it does in so many Indian buildings, I obtain a fine view of the lower slopes of the sacred hill. Its strange outline is bathed in the early morning sunlight.

The Maharshi addresses me again:

"Will it be clear if it is put in this way? All human beings are ever wanting happiness, untainted with sorrow. They want to grasp a happiness which will not come to an end. The instinct is a true one. But have you ever been struck by the fact that they love their own selves most?"

"Well?"

"Now relate that to the fact that they are ever desirous of attaining happiness through one means or another, through drink or through religion, and you are provided with a clue to the real nature of man."

"I fail to see........"

The tone of his voice becomes higher.

"Man's real nature is happiness. Happiness is inborn in the true Self. His search for happiness is an unconscious search for his true Self. The true Self is imperishable; therefore when a man finds it, he finds a happiness which does not come to an end."

"But the world is so unhappy?"

"Yes, but that is because the world is ignorant of its true Self. All men, without exception, are consciously or unconsciously seeking for it."

"Even the wicked, the brutal and the criminal?" I ask.

"Even they sin because they are trying to find the Self's happiness in every sin which they commit. This striving is instinctive in man, but they do not know that they are really seeking their true selves, and so they try these wicked ways first as a means to happiness. Of course, they are wrong ways, for a man's acts are reflected back to him."

"So we shall feel lasting happiness when we know this true Self?"

The other nods his head.

A slanting ray of sunshine falls through the unglazed window upon the Maharshi's face. There is serenity in that unruffled brow, there is contentment around that firm mouth, there is a shine-like peace in those lustrous eyes. His unlined countenance does not belie his revelatory words.

What does the Maharshi mean by these apparently simple sentences? The interpreter has conveyed their outward meaning to me in English, yes, but there is a deeper purport which he cannot convey. I know that I must discover that for myself. The Sage seems to speak, not as a philosopher, not as a pundit trying to explain his own doctrine, but rather out of the depth of his own heart. Are these words the marks of his own fortunate experience?

"What exactly is this Self of which you speak? If what you say is true, then there must be another self in man."

His lips curve in smile for a moment.

"Can a man be possessed of two identities, two selves?" he makes answer. "To understand this matter it is first necessary for a man to analyse himself. Because it has long been his habit to think as others think, he has never faced his 'I' in the true manner. He has not a correct picture of himself; he has too long identified himself with the body and the brain. Therefore, I tell you to pursue this enquiry, 'Who am I?'"

He pauses to let these words soak into me. I listen eagerly to his next sentences.

"You ask me to describe this true Self to you. What can be said? It is That out of which the sense of the personal 'I' arises, and into which it shall have to disappear."

"Disappear?" I echo back. "How can one lose the feeling of one's personality?"

"The first and foremost of all thoughts, the primeval thought in the mind of every man, is the thought 'I'. It is only after the birth of this thought that any other thoughts can arise at all. It is only after the first personal pronoun 'I' has arisen in the mind that the personal pronoun 'you' can make its appearance. If you could mentally follow the 'I' thread until it leads you back to its source, you would discover that, just as it is the first thought to appear, so is it the last to disappear. This is a matter which can be experienced."

"You mean that it is perfectly possible to conduct such a mental investigation into oneself?"

"Assuredly! It is possible to go inwards until the last thought 'I' gradually vanishes."

"What is left?" I query. "Will a man then become quite unconscious, or will he become an idiot?"

"Not so! On the contrary, he will attain that consciousness which is immortal, and he will become truly wise, when he has awakened to his true Self, which is the real nature of man."

"But surely the sense of 'I' must also pertain to that?" I persist.

"The sense of 'I' pertains to the person, the body and the brain," replies the Maharshi calmly. "When a man knows his true Self for the first time, something else arises from the depths of his being and takes possession of him. That something is behind the mind; it is infinite, divine, eternal. Some people call it the kingdom of heaven, others call it the soul, still others name it *Nirvana*, and we Hindus call it Liberation; you may give it what name you wish. When this happens, a man has not really lost himself; rather, he has found himself."

As the last word falls from the interpreter's lips there flashes across my mind those memorable words which were uttered by a wandering Teacher in Galilee, words which have puzzled so many good persons: *Whosoever shall seek to save his life shall lose it: and whosoever shall lose his life shall preserve it.*

How strangely similar are the two sentences! Yet the Indian Sage has arrived at the thought in his own non-Christian way, through a psychological path which seems exceedingly difficult and appears unfamiliar.

The Maharshi speaks again, his words breaking into my thoughts:

"Unless and until a man embarks upon this quest of the true Self, doubt and uncertainty will follow his footsteps throughout life. The greatest kings and statesmen try to rule others, when in their heart of hearts they know that they cannot rule themselves. Yet the greatest power is at the command of the man who has penetrated to his inmost depth. There are men of giant intellects who spend their lives gathering knowledge about many things. Ask these men if they have solved the mystery of man, if they have conquered themselves, and they will hang their heads in shame. What is the use of knowing about everything else when you do not yet know who you are? Men avoid this enquiry into the true Self, but what else is there so worthy to be undertaken?"

"That is such a difficult, superhuman task," I comment.

The Sage gives an almost imperceptible shrug of his shoulders.

"The question of its possibility is a matter of one's own experience. The difficulty is less real than you think."

"For us, who are active, practical Westerners, such introspections . . . . . ?" I begin doubtfully and leave my sentence trailing in midair.

The Maharshi bends down to light a fresh joss stick, which will replace one whose red spark is dying out.

"The realization of truth is the same for both Indians and Europeans. Admittedly the way to it may be harder for those who are engrossed in worldly life, but even then one can and must conquer. The current induced during meditation can be kept up by habit, by practising to do so. Then one can perform his work and activities in that very current itself; there will be no break. Thus, too there will be no difference between meditation and external activities. If you meditate on this question, 'Who am I?', if you begin to perceive that neither the body nor the brain nor the desires are really you, then the very attitude of enquiry will eventually draw the answer to you out of the depths of your own being; it will come to you of its own accord as a deep realization."

Again I ponder his words.

"Know the real Self," he continues, "and then the truth will shine forth within your heart like sunshine. The mind will become untroubled and real happiness will flood it; for happiness and the true self are identical. You will have no more doubts once you attain this Self-awareness."

He turns his head and fixes his gaze at the far end of the hall. I know then that he has reached his conversational limit. Thus ends our last talk and I congratulate myself that I have drawn him out of the shell of taciturnity before my departure.

§

I leave him and wander away to a quiet spot in the jungle, where I spend most of the day among my notes and books. When dusk falls I return to the hall, for within an hour or two a pony-carriage or a bullock-cart will arrive to bear me away from the hermitage.

Burning incense makes the air odorous. The Maharshi has been half reclining under the waving *punkah* as I enter but he soon sits up and assumes his favourite attitude. He sits with legs crossed, the right foot placed on the left thigh and the left foot merely folded beneath the right thigh. I remember being shown a similar position by Brama, the *yogi* who lives near Madras, who called it "The Comfortable Posture." It is really a half-Buddha posture and quite easy to do. The Maharshi, as is his wont, holds his chin with his right hand and rests the elbow on a knee; next he gazes attentively at me but remains quite silent. On the floor beside him I notice his gourd-shell, water jug and his bamboo staff. They are his sole earthly possessions, apart from the strip of loin-cloth. What a mute commentary on our Western spirit of acquisitiveness!

His eyes, always shining, steadily become more glazed and fixed; his body sets into a rigid pose; his head trembles slightly and then comes to rest. A few more minutes and I can plainly see that he has re-entered the trance like condition in which he was when I first met him. How strange that our parting shall repeat our meeting! Someone brings his face close to mine and whispers in my ear, "The Maharshi has gone into holy trance. It is useless now to talk."

A hush falls upon the little company. The minutes slowly pass but the silence only deepens. I am not religious but I can no more resist the feeling of increasing awe which begins to grip my mind than a bee can resist a flower in all its luscious bloom. The hall is becoming pervaded with a subtle, intangible and indefinable power which affects me deeply. I feel, without doubt and without hesitation, that the centre of this mysterious power is no other than the Maharshi himself.

His eyes shine with astonishing brilliance. Strange sensations begin to arise in me. Those lustrous orbs seem to be peering into the inmost recesses of my soul. In a peculiar way, I feel aware of everything he can see in my heart. His mysterious glance penetrates my thoughts, my emotions and my desires; I am helpless before it. At first this disconcerting gaze troubles me; I become vaguely uneasy. I feel that he has perceived pages that belong to a past which I have forgotten. He knows it all, I am certain. I am powerless to escape; somehow, I do not want to, either. Some curious intimation of future benefit forces me to endure that pitiless gaze.

And so he continues to catch the feeble quality of my soul for a while, to perceive my motley past, to sense the mixed emotions which have drawn me this way and that. But I feel that he understands also what mind-devastating quest has impelled me to leave the common way and seek out such men as he.

There comes a perceptible change in the telepathic current which plays between us, the while my eyes blink frequently but his remain without the least tremor. I become aware that he is definitely linking my own mind with his; that he is provoking my heart into that state of starry calm which he seems perpetually to enjoy. In this extraordinary peace, I find a sense of exaltation and lightness. Time seems to stand still. My heart is released from its burden of care. Never again, I feel, shall the bitterness of anger and the melancholy of unsatisfied desire afflict me. I realize deeply that the profound instinct which is innate in the race, which bids man look up, which encourages him to hope on, and which sustains him when life has darkened, is a true instinct, for the essence of being is good. In this beautiful, entranced silence, when the clock stands still and the sorrows and errors of the past seem like trivialities, my mind is being submerged in that of the Maharshi and wisdom is now at its perihelion. What is this man's gaze but a thaumaturgic wand, which evokes a hidden world of unexpected splendour before my profane eyes?

I have sometimes asked myself why these disciples have been staying around the Sage for years, with few conversations, fewer comforts and no external activities to attract them. Now I begin to understand — not by thought but by lightning like illumination — that through all those years they have been receiving a deep and silent reward.

Hitherto, everyone in the hall has been hushed to a deathlike stillness. At length, someone quietly rises and passes out. He is followed by another, and then another, until all have gone.

I am alone with the Maharshi! Never before has this happened. His eyes begin to change; they narrow down to pinpoints. The effect is curiously like the "stopping-down" in the focus of a camera lens. There comes a tremendous increase in the intense gleam which shines between the lids, now almost closed. Suddenly, my body seems to disappear, and we are both out in space!

It is a crucial moment. I hesitate — and decide to break this enchanter's spell. Decision brings power and once again I am back in the flesh, back in the hall.

No word passes from him to me. I collect my faculties, look at the clock, and rise quietly. The hour of departure has arrived.

I bow my head in farewell. The Sage silently acknowledges the gesture. I utter a few words of thanks. Again, he silently nods his head.

I linger reluctantly at the threshold. Outside, I hear the tinkle of a bell. The bullock cart has arrived. Once more I raise my hands, palms touching.

And so we part.

In a Jungle Hermitage

THERE ARE MOMENTS UNFORGETTABLE WHICH mark themselves in golden figures upon the calendar of our years. Such a moment comes to me now, as I walk into the hall of the Maharshi.

He sits as usual upon the magnificent tiger skin which covers the centre of his divan. The joss sticks burn slowly away on a little table near him, spreading the penetrating fragrance of incense around the hall. Not today is he remote from men and wrapped up in some trance-like spiritual absorption as on that strange occasion when I first visited him. His eyes are clearly open to this world and glance at me comprehendingly as I bow, and his mouth is stretched in a kindly smile of welcome.

Squatting at a respectful distance from their master are a few disciples; otherwise the long hall is bare. One of them pulls the punkah fan which flaps lazily through the heavy air.

In my heart I know that I come as one seeking to take up the position of a disciple, and that there will be no rest for my mind until I hear the Maharshi's decision. It is true that I live in a great hope of being accepted, for that which sent me scurrying out of Bombay to this place came as an absolute command, a decisive and authoritative injunction from a supernormal region. In a few words I dispose of the preliminary explanations, and then put my request briefly and bluntly to the Maharshi.

He continues to smile at me, but says nothing.

I repeat my question with some emphasis.

There is another protracted pause, but at length he answers me, disdaining to call for the services of an interpreter and expressing himself directly in English.

"What is all this talk of Masters and disciples? All these differences exist only from the disciple's standpoint. To the one who has realized the true Self there is neither Master nor disciple. Such a one regards all people with equal eye."

I am slightly conscious of an initial rebuff, and though I press my request in other ways, the Maharshi refuses to yield on the point. But in the end he does say:

"You must find the Master within you, within your own spiritual Self. You must regard his body in the same way that he himself regards it; the body is not his true Self."

It begins to voice itself in my thoughts that the Maharshi is not to be drawn into giving me a direct affirmative response, and that the answer I seek must be found in some other way, doubtless in the subtle, obscure manner at which he hints. So I let the matter drop and our talk then turns to the outward and material side of my visit.

I spend the afternoon making some arrangements for a protracted stay.

§

The ensuing weeks absorb me into a strange, unwonted life. My days are spent in the hall of the Maharshi, where I slowly pick up the unrelated fragments of his wisdom and the faint clues to the answer I seek; my nights continue as heretofore in torturing sleeplessness, with my body stretched out on a blanket laid on the hard earthen floor of a hastily built hut.

This humble abode stands about three hundred feet away from the hermitage. Its thick walls are composed of thinly plastered earth, but the roof is solidly tiled to withstand the monsoon rains. The ground around it is virgin bush, somewhat thickly overgrown, being in fact the fringe of the jungle which stretches away to the west. The rugged landscape reveals Nature in all her own wild uncultivated grandeur. Cactus hedges are scattered numerously and irregularly around, the spines of these prickly plants looking like coarse needles. Beyond them the jungle drops a curtain of scrub bush and stunted trees upon the land. To the north rises the gaunt figure of the mountain, a mass of metallic-tinted rocks and brown soil. To the south lies a long pool, whose placid water has attracted me to the spot, and whose banks are bordered with clumps of trees holding families of grey and brown monkeys.

Each day is a duplicate of the one before. I rise early in the morning and watch the jungle dawn turn from grey to green and then to gold. Next comes a plunge into the water and a swift swim up and down the pool, making as much noise as I possibly can so as to scare away lurking snakes. Then, dressing, shaving, and the only luxury I can secure in this place — three cups of deliciously refreshing tea.

"Master, the pot of tea-water is ready," says Rajoo, my hired boy. From an initial total ignorance of the English language, he has acquired that much, and more, under my occasional tuition. As a servant he is a gem, for he will scour up and down the little township with optimistic determination in quest of the strange articles and foods for which his Western employer speculatively sends him, or he will hover outside the Maharshi's hall in discreet silence during meditation hours, should he happen to come along for orders at such times. But as a cook he is unable to comprehend Western taste, which seems a queer distorted thing to him. After a few painful experiments, I myself take charge of the more serious culinary arrangements, reducing my labour by reducing my solid meals to a single one each day. Tea, taken thrice daily, becomes both my solitary earthly joy and the mainstay of my energy. Rajoo stands in the sunshine and watches with wonderment my addiction to the glorious brown brew. His body shines in the hard yellow light like polished ebony, for he is a true son of the black Dravidians, the primal inhabitants of India.

After breakfast comes my quiet lazy stroll to the hermitage, a halt for a couple of minutes beside the sweet rose bushes in the compound garden, which is fenced in by bamboo posts, or a rest under the drooping fronds of palm trees whose heads are heavy with coconuts. It is a beautiful experience to wander around the hermitage garden before the sun has waxed in power and to see and smell the variegated flowers.

And then I enter the hall, bow before the Maharshi and quietly sit down on folded legs. I may read or write for a while, or engage in conversation with one or two of the other men, or tackle the Maharshi on some point, or plunge into meditation for an hour along the lines which the Sage has indicated, although evening usually constitutes the time specially assigned to meditation in the hall. But whatever I am doing I never fail to become gradually aware of the mysterious atmosphere of the place, of the benign radiations which steadily percolate into my brain. I enjoy an ineffable tranquillity merely by sitting for a while in the neighbourhood of the Maharshi. By careful observation and frequent analysis I arrive in time at the complete certitude that reciprocal inter-influence arises whenever our presences neighbour each other. The thing is most subtle. But it is quite unmistakable.

At eleven I return to the hut for the midday meal and a rest and then go back to the hall to repeat my programme of the morning. I vary my meditations and conversations sometimes by roaming the countryside or descending on the little township to make further explorations of the colossal temple.

From time to time the Maharshi unexpectedly visits me at the hut after finishing his own lunch. I seize the opportunity to plague him with further questions, which he patiently answers in terse epigrammatic phrases, clipped so short as rarely to constitute complete sentences. But once, when I propound some fresh problem, he makes no answer. Instead, he gazes out towards the jungle covered hills which stretch to the horizon and remains motionless. Many minutes pass but still his eyes are fixed, his presence remote. I am quite unable to discern whether his attention is being given to some invisible psychic being in the distance or whether it is being turned on some inward preoccupation. At first I wonder whether he has heard me, but in the tense silence which ensues, and which I feel unable or unwilling to break, a force greater than my rationalistic mind commences to awe me until it ends by overwhelming me.

The realization forces itself through my wonderment that all my questions are moves in an endless game, the play of thoughts which possess no limit to their extent; that somewhere within me there is a well of certitude which can provide me all the waters of truth I require; and that it will be better to cease my questioning and attempt to realize the tremendous potencies of my own spiritual nature. So I remain silent and wait.

For almost half an hour the Maharshi's eyes continue to stare straight in front of him in a fixed, unmoving gaze. He appears to have forgotten me, but I am perfectly aware that the sublime realization which has suddenly fallen upon me is nothing else than a spreading ripple of telepathic radiation from this mysterious and imperturbable man.

On another visit he finds me in a pessimistic mood. He tells me of the glorious goal which waits for the man who takes to the way he has shown.

"But, Maharshi, this path is full of difficulties and I am so conscious of my own weakness," I plead.

"That is the surest way to handicap oneself," he answers unmoved, "this burdening of one's mind with the fear of failure and the thought of one's failings."

"Yet if it is true — ?" I persist.

"It is not true. The greatest error of a man is to think that he is weak by nature, evil by nature. Every man is divine and strong in his real nature. What are weak and evil are his habits, his desires and thoughts, but not himself."

His words come as an invigorating tonic. They refresh and inspire me. From another man's lips, from some lesser and feebler soul, I would refuse to accept them at such worth and would persist in refuting them. But an inward monitor assures me that the Sage speaks out of the depth of a great and authentic spiritual experience, and not as some theorising philosopher mounted on the thin stilts of speculation.

Another time, when we are discussing the West, I make the retort:

"It is easy for you to attain and keep spiritual serenity in this jungle retreat, where there is nothing to disturb or distract you."

"When the goal is reached, when you know the Knower, there is no difference between living in a house in London and living in the solitude of a jungle," comes the calm rejoinder.

And once I criticise the Indians for their neglect of material development. To my surprise the Maharshi frankly admits the accusation.

"It is true. We are a backward race. But we are a people with few wants. Our society needs improving, but we are contented with much fewer things than your people. So to be backward is not to mean that we are less happy."

How has the Maharshi arrived at the strange power and stranger outlook which he possesses? Bit by bit, from his own reluctant lips and from those of his disciples, I piece together a fragmentary pattern of his life story.*

He was born in 1879 in a village about thirty miles distant from Madura, which is a noted South Indian town possessing one of the largest temples in the country. His father followed some avocation connected with law and came of good *brahmin* stock. His father appears to have been an extremely charitable man who fed and clothed many poor persons. The boy eventually passed to Madura to carry on his education, and it was here that he picked up the rudiments of English in a school conducted by American missionaries.

At first young Ramana was fond of play and sport. He wrestled, boxed and swam dangerous rivers. He betrayed no special interest in religious or philosophical concerns. The only exceptional thing in his life at the time was a tendency to a condition of sleep so profound that the most disturbing interruptions could not awaken him. His schoolmates eventually discovered this and took advantage of it to sport with him. During the daytime they were afraid of his quick punch, but at night they would come into his bedroom, take him into the playground, beat his body and box his ears, and then lead him back to bed. He was quite unconscious of these experiences and had no remembrance of them in the mornings.

The psychologist who has correctly understood the nature of sleep will find in this account of the boy's abnormal depth of attention, sufficient indication of the mystical nature which he possessed.

---

*The reader is directed to the book, *Self-Realisation* by B.V. Narasimha Swami which gives the detailed life story of the Maharshi.

One day a relative came to Madura and in answer to Ramana's question, mentioned that he had just returned from a pilgrimage to Arunachala. The name stirred some slumbering depths in the boy's mind, thrilling him with peculiar expectations which he could not understand. He enquired as to the whereabouts of Arunachala and ever after found himself haunted by thoughts of it. It seemed to be of paramount importance to him, yet he could not even explain to himself why Arunachala should mean anything more to him than the dozens of other sacred places which are scattered over India.

He continued his studies at the Mission school without showing any special aptitude for them, although he always evinced a fair degree of intelligence in his work. But when he was seventeen, destiny, with swift and sudden stroke, got into action and thrust its hands through the even tenor of his days.

He suddenly left the school and completely abandoned all his studies. He gave no notice to his teachers or to his relatives, and told no one before the event actually occurred. What was the reason of this unpromising change, which cast a cloud upon his future worldly prospectus?

The reason was satisfying enough to himself, though it might have seemed mind-perplexing to others. For life, which in the ultimate is the teacher of men, set the young student on another course than that which his school teachers had assigned him. And the change came in a curious way about six weeks before he dropped his studies and disappeared from Madura forever.

He was sitting alone one day in his room when a sudden and inexplicable fear of death took hold of him. He became acutely aware that he was going to die, although outwardly he was in good health. The thing was a psychological phenomenon, because there was no apparent reason why he should die. Yet he became obsessed with this notion and immediately began to prepare for the coming event.

He stretched his body prone upon the floor, fixed his limbs in the rigidity of a corpse, closed his eyes and mouth, and finally held his breath. "Well, then" said I to myself, "this body is dead. It will be carried stiff to the burning ground and then reduced to ashes. But with the death of the body, am 'I' dead? Is the body 'I'? This body is now silent and stiff. But I continue to feel the full force of my Self apart from its condition."

Those are the words which the Maharshi used in describing the weird experience through which he passed. What happened next is difficult to understand, though easy to describe. He seemed to fall into a profound conscious trance wherein he became merged into the very source of selfhood, the very essence of Being. He understood quite clearly that the body was a thing apart and that the 'I' remained untouched by death. The true Self was very real, but it was so deep down in man's nature that hitherto he had ignored it.

Ramana emerged from this amazing experience an utterly changed youth. He lost most of his interest in studies, sports, friends, and so on, because his chief interest was now centred in the sublime consciousness of the true Self which he had found so unexpectedly. Fear of death vanished as mysteriously as it came. He enjoyed an inward serenity and a spiritual strength which have never since left him. Formerly he had been quick to retaliate at the other boys when they had chaffed him or attempted to take liberties, but now he put up with everything quite meekly. He suffered unjust acts with indifference and bore himself among others with complete humility. He gave up old habits and tried to be alone as much as possible, for then he would sink into meditation and surrender himself to the absorbing current of divine consciousness, which constantly drew his attention inwards.

These profound changes in his character were, of course, noticed by others. One day when the boy was doing his homework his elder brother who was in the same room found him sinking into meditation with closed eyes. The school books and papers were tossed across the room in disgust. The brother was so annoyed at this neglect of studies that he jeered at him with sharp words:

"What business has a fellow like you here? If you want to behave like a *yogi*, why are you studying for a career?"

Young Ramana was deeply stung by these words. He immediately realized their truth and silently decided to act upon them. His father was dead and he knew that his uncle and other brothers would take care of his mother. Truly he had no business there. And back into his mind there flashed the name which had haunted him, the name whose very syllables fascinated him, the name of Arunachala. Thither would he go, although why he should select that place he was quite unable to say. But an impelling urgency arose within him and formed the decision for him of its own accord. It was entirely unpremeditated.

"I was literally charmed here," said the Maharshi to me. "The same force which drew you to this place from Bombay, drew me to it from Madura."

And so young Ramana, feeling this inner pull within his heart, left friends, family, school and studies and took the road which eventually brought him to Arunachala and to a still profounder spiritual attainment. He left behind a brief farewell letter, which is still preserved in the hermitage. Its flourishing Tamil characters read as follows:

I have in search of my Father and in obedience to His command, started from here. This is only embarking on a virtuous enterprise. Therefore none need grieve over this affair. To trace this out, no money need be spent.

With three rupees in his pocket and an utter ignorance of the world, he set out on the journey into the interior of the South. The amazing incidents which marked that journey prove conclusively that some mysterious power was protecting and guiding him. When at last he arrived at his destination, he was utterly destitute and among total strangers. But the emotion of total renunciation was burning strong within him. Such was the youth's scorn for all earthly possessions, that he flung his robe aside and took up his meditative posture in the temple precincts quite nude. A priest observed this and remonstrated with him, but to no purpose. Other shocked priests came along, and after vehement efforts, forced a concession from the youth. He consented to wear a loin-cloth and that is all he has ever worn to this day.

For six months he occupied various spots in the precincts, never going anywhere else. He lived on some rice which was brought him once a day by a priest who was struck by the precocious behaviour of the youth. For Ramana spent the entire day plunged in mystical trances and spiritual ecstasies so profound that he was entirely oblivious of the world around him. When some rough Moslem youths flung mud at him and ran away, he was quite unaware of the fact until some hours later. He felt no resentment against them in his heart.

The stream of pilgrims who descended on the temple made it difficult for him to obtain the seclusion he desired. So he left the place and moved to a quiet shrine set in the fields some distance from the village. Here he continued to stay for a year and a half. He was satisfied with the food brought by the few people who visited this shrine.

Throughout this time he spoke to no one; indeed, he never opened his lips to talk until three years passed since his arrival in the district. This was not because he had taken a vow of silence, but because his inner monitor urged him to concentrate all his energy and attention upon his spiritual life. When his mystic goal was attained the inhibition was no longer necessary and he began to talk again, though the Maharshi has remained an extremely taciturn man.

He kept his identity a complete secret, but by a chain of coincidences, his mother discovered his whereabouts two years after his disappearance. She set out for the place with her eldest son and tearfully pleaded with him to return home. The lad refused to budge. When tears failed to persuade him, she began to upbraid him for his indifference. Eventually he wrote down a reply on a piece of paper to the effect that a higher power controls the fate of men and that whatever she did could not change his destiny. He concluded by advising her to accept the situation and to cease moaning about it. And so she had to yield to his decision.

When, through this incident, people began to intrude on his seclusion in order to stare at the youthful *yogi*, he left the place and climbed up the Hill of the Holy Beacon and made his residence in a large cavern, where he lived for several years. There are quite a few other caves on this hill and each one shelters holy men or *yogis*. But the cave which sheltered young Ramana was noteworthy because it also contained the tomb of a great *yogi* of the past.

Cremation is the usual custom of the Hindus in disposing of their dead, but it is prohibited in the case of a *yogi* who is believed to have made the highest attainment, because it is also believed that the vital breath or unseen life-current remains in his body for thousands of years and renders the flesh exempt from corruption. In such a case the *yogi*'s body is bathed and anointed and then placed in a tomb in a sitting posture with crossed legs, as though he was still plunged in meditation. The entrance to the tomb is sealed with a heavy stone and then cemented over. Usually the mausoleum becomes a place of pilgrimage. There exists still another reason why great *yogi*s are buried and not cremated and that is because of the belief that their bodies do not need to be purified during their lifetimes.

It is interesting to consider that caves have always been a favourite residence of *yogi*s and holy men. The ancients consecrated them to the gods; Zoroaster, the founder of the Parsi faith, practised his meditations in a cave, while Muhammad received his religious experiences in a cave also. The Indian *yogi*s have very good reasons for preferring caves or subterranean retreats when better places are not available. For here they can find shelter from the vicissitudes of weather and from the rapid changes of temperature which divide days from nights in the tropics. There is less light and noise to disturb their meditations. And breathing the confined atmosphere of a cave causes the appetite to diminish markedly, thus conducing to a minimum of bodily cares.

Still another reason which may have attracted Ramana to this particular cave on the Hill of the Holy Beacon was the beauty of its outlook. One can stand on a projecting spur adjoining the cave and see the little township stretched out flat in the distant plain, with the giant temple rising as its centrepiece. Far beyond the plain stands a long line of hills which frontier a charming panorama of Nature.

Anyway, Ramana lived in this somewhat gloomy cavern for several years, engaged in his mysterious meditations and plunged in profound trances. He was not a *yogi* in the orthodox sense, for he had never practised under any teacher. The inner path which he followed was simply a track leading to Self-knowledge; it was laid down by what he conceived to be the divine monitor within him.

In 1905 plague appeared in the locality. The dread visitant was probably carried into the district by some pilgrim to the temple of Arunachala. It devastated the population so fiercely that almost everyone left the little township and fled in terror to safer villages or towns. So quiet did the deserted place become that tigers and leopards came out of their lurking dens in the jungle and moved openly through the streets. But, though they must have roamed the hillside many times, for it stood in their path to the township, though they must have passed and repassed the Maharshi's cave, he refused to leave, but remained as calm and unmoved as ever.

By this time, the young hermit had involuntarily acquired a solitary disciple, who had become very much attached to him and persisted in staying by his side and attending to his needs. The man is now dead. But the legend has been handed down to other disciples that at nights a large tiger came to the cave, stood in front of Ramana and peacefully departed.

There is a widespread notion throughout India that *yogis* and *fakirs* who live in the jungles or on the mountains exposed to danger from lions, tigers, snakes and other wild creatures, move unharmed and untouched if they have attained a sufficient degree of *yogic* power. Another story about Ramana told how he was once sitting in the afternoon outside the narrow entrance to his abode when a large cobra came swishing through the rocks and stopped in front of him. It raised its body and spread out its hood, but the hermit did not attempt to move. The two beings — man and beast — faced each other for some minutes, gaze meeting gaze. In the end the snake withdrew and left him unharmed, although it was within striking distance.

The austere lonely life of this strange young man closed its first phase with his firm and permanent establishment in the deepest point of his own spirit. Seclusion was no longer an imperative need, but he continued to live at the cave until the visit of an illustrious *brahmin* pundit, Ganapati Sastri, proved another turning point of his outer life, which was now to enter on a more social period. The pundit had recently come to stay near the temple for study and meditation. He heard by chance that there was a very young *yogi* on the hill and out of curiosity he went in search of him. When he found Ramana, the latter was staring fixedly at the sun. It was not at all uncommon for the hermit to keep his eyes on the dazzling sun for some hours till it disappeared below the western horizon.

The glaring light of the rays of an afternoon sun in India can hardly be appreciated by a European who has never experienced it. I remember once, when I had set out to climb the steep ascent of the hill at a wrong hour, being caught without shelter by the full glare of the sun at midday on my return journey. I staggered and reeled about like a drunken man for quite a time. So the feat of young Ramana in enduring the merciless glare of the sun, with face uplifted and eyes unflinching, may therefore be better evaluated.

The pundit had studied all the chief books of Hindu wisdom for a dozen years and had undergone rigorous penances in an endeavour to reach some tangible spiritual benefit, but he was still afflicted by doubts and perplexities. He put a question to Ramana and after fifteen minutes received a reply which amazed him with its wisdom. He put further questions, involving his own philosophical and spiritual problems, and was still more astounded at the clearing up of perplexities which had troubled him for years. As a result he prostrated himself before the young hermit and became a disciple. Sastri had his own group of followers in the town of Vellore and he went back later and told them that he had found a Maharshi (Great Sage or Seer), because the latter was undoubtedly a man of the highest spiritual realization whose teachings were so original that the pundit had found nothing exactly like them in any book he had read. From that time the title of Maharshi began to be applied to young Ramana by cultured people, although the common folk wanted to worship him as a divine being when his existence and character became better known to them. But the Maharshi strongly forbade every manifestation of such worship in his presence. Among themselves and in private talk with me, most of his devotees and people in the locality insist on calling him a god.

A small group of disciples attached themselves to the Maharshi in time. They built a wooden frame bungalow on a lower spur of the hill and persuaded him to live in it with them. In different years his mother had paid him short visits and became reconciled to his vocation. When death parted her from her eldest son and other relatives, she came to the Maharshi and begged him to let her live with him. He consented. She spent the six years of life which were left to her at his side, and finished up by becoming an ardent disciple of her own son. In return for the hospitality which was given to her in the little hermitage, she used to cook and serve food for all his disciples.

When the old lady died, her remains were buried at the foot of the hill and some of the Maharshi's devotees built a small shrine over the place. Here, ever-burning sacred lamps glow in memory of this woman, who gave a great Sage to mankind, and little heaps of scented jasmines and marigolds, snatched from their stalks, are thrown on a tiny altar in offering to her spirit.

The efflux of time spread the reputation of the Maharshi throughout the locality, so that pilgrims to the temple were often induced to go up the hill and see him before they returned home. Quite recently the Maharshi yielded to incessant requests and consented to grace the new and large hall which was built at the foot of the hill as a residence for him and his disciples.

The Maharshi has never asked for anything but food, and consistently refuses to handle money. Whatever else has came to him has been voluntarily pressed upon him by others. During those early years when he tried to live a solitary existence, when he built a wall of almost impenetrable silent reserve around himself whilst he was perfecting his spiritual powers, he did not disdain to leave his cave with a begging bowl in hand and wander to the village for some food whenever the pangs of hunger stirred his body. An old widow took pity on him and thenceforth regularly supplied him with food, eventually insisting on bringing it up to his cave. Thus his venture of faith in leaving his comfortable middle-class home was, in a measure, justified, at any rate to the extent that whatever powers there be have ensured his shelter and food. Many gifts have since been offered him, but as a rule he turns them away.

When a gang of dacoits broke into the hall one night not long ago and searched the place for money, they were unable to find more than a few rupees, which was in the care of the man who superintended the purchase of food. The robbers were so angry at this disappointment that they belaboured the Maharshi with stout clubs, severely marking his body. The Sage not only bore their attack patiently, but requested them to take a meal before they departed. He actually offered them some food. He had no hate towards them in his heart. Pity for their spiritual ignorance was the sole emotion they aroused. He let them escape freely, but within a year they were caught while committing another crime elsewhere and received stiff sentences of penal servitude.

Not a few Western minds will inevitably consider that this life of the Maharshi's is a wasted one. But perhaps it may be good for us to have a few men who sit apart from our world of unending activity and survey it for us from afar. The onlooker may see more of the game and sometimes he gets a truer perspective. It may also be that a jungle Sage, with self lying conquered at his feet, is not inferior to a worldly fool who is blown hither and thither by every circumstance.

§

Day after day brings its fresh indications of the greatness of this man. Among the strangely diversified company of human beings who pass through the hermitage, a pariah stumbles into the hall in some great agony of soul or circumstances and pours out his tribulation at the Maharshi's feet. The Sage does not reply, for his silence and reserve are habitual; one can easily count up the number of words he uses in a single day. Instead, he gazes quietly at the suffering man, whose cries gradually diminish until he leaves the hall two hours later a more serene and stronger man.

I am learning to see that this is the Maharshi's way of helping others, this unobtrusive, silent and steady outpouring of healing vibrations into troubled souls, this mysterious telepathic process for which science will one day be required to account.

A cultured *brahmin*, college-bred, arrives with his questions. One can never be certain whether the Sage will make a verbal response or not, for often he is eloquent enough without opening his lips. But today he is in a communicative mood and a few of his terse phrases, packed with profound meanings as they usually are, open many vistas of thought for the visitor.

A large group of visitors and devotees are in the hall when someone arrives with the news that a certain man, whose criminal reputation is a byword in the little township, is dead. Immediately there is some discussion about him and, as is the wont of human nature, various people engaged in recalling some of his crimes and the more dastardly phases of his character. When the hubbub has subsided and the discussion appears to have ended, the Maharshi opens his mouth for the first time and quietly observes:

"Yes, but he kept himself very clean, for he bathed two or three times a day!"

A peasant and his family have travelled over some hundred miles to pay silent homage to the Sage. He is totally illiterate, knows little beyond his daily work, his religious rites and ancestral superstitions. He has heard from someone that there is a god in human form living at the foot of the Hill of the Holy Beacon. He sits on the floor quietly after having prostrated himself three times. He firmly believes that some blessing of spirit or fortune will come to him as a result of this journey. His wife moves gracefully to his side and drops to the floor. She is clothed in a purple robe which flows smoothly from head to ankles and is then tucked into her waist. Her sleek and smooth hair is glossy with scented oil. Her daughter accompanies her. She is a pretty girl whose ankle-rings click in consort as she steps into the hall. And she follows the charming custom of wearing a white flower behind her ear.

The little family stay for a few hours, hardly speaking, and gaze in reverence at the Maharshi. It is clear that his mere presence provides them with spiritual assurance, emotional felicity and, most paradoxical of all, renewed faith in their creed. For the Sage treats all creeds alike, regards them all as significant and sincere expressions of a great experience, and honours Jesus no less than Krishna.

On my left squats an old man of seventy-five. A quid of betel is comfortably tucked in his cheek, a Sanskrit book lies between his hands, and his heavy lidded eyes stare meditatively at the bold print. He is a *brahmin* who was a station-master near Madras for many years. He retired from the railway service at sixty and soon after his wife died. He took opportunity thus presented of realising some long deferred aspirations. For fourteen years he travelled about the country on pilgrimage to the sages, saints and *yogis*, trying to find one whose teachings and personality were sufficiently appealing to him. He had circled India thrice, but no such master had been discoverable. He had set up a very individual standard apparently. When we met and compared notes he lamented his failure. His rugged honest face, carved by wrinkles into dark furrows, appealed to me. He was not an intellectual man, but simple and quite intuitive. Being considerably younger than he, I felt it incumbent on me to give the old man some good advice! His surprising response was a request to become his master! "Your master is not far off," I told him and conducted him straight to the Maharshi. It did not take long for him to agree with me and become an enthusiastic devotee of the Sage.

Another man in the hall is bespectacled, silken clad and prosperous looking. He is a judge who has taken advantage of a law vacation to pay a visit to the Maharshi. He is a keen disciple and strong admirer and never fails to come at least once a year. This cultured, refined and highly educated gentleman squats democratically among a group of Tamils who are poor, naked to the waist and smeared with oil, so that their bodies glisten like varnished ebony. That which brings them together destroys the insufferable snobbishness of caste, and produces unity, is that which caused Princes and Rajahs to come from afar in ancient times to consult the forest *rishis* — the deep recognition that true wisdom is worth the sacrifice of superficial differences.

A young woman with a gaily attired child enters and prostrates herself in veneration before the Sage. Some profound problems of life are being discussed, so she sits in silence, not venturing to take part in intellectual conversation. Learning is not regarded as an ornament for Hindu women and she knows little outside the purlieus of culinary and domestic matters. But she knows when she is in the presence of undeniable greatness.

With the descent of dusk comes the time for a general group meditation in the hall. Not infrequently the Maharshi will signal the time by entering, so gently as occasionally to be unnoticed, the trance-like abstraction wherein he locks his senses against the world outside. During these daily meditations in the potent neighbourhood of the Sage, I have learnt how to carry my thoughts inward to an ever deepening point. It is impossible to be in frequent contact with him without becoming lit up inwardly, as it were, mentally illumined by a sparkling ray from his spiritual orb. Again and again I become conscious that he is drawing my mind into his own atmosphere during these periods of quiet repose. And it is at such times that one begins to understand why the silences of this man are more significant than his utterances. His quiet unhurried poise veils a dynamic attainment, which can powerfully affect a person without the medium of audible speech or visible action. There are moments when I feel this power of his so greatly that I know he has only to issue the most disturbing command and I will readily obey it. But the Maharshi is the last person in the world to place his followers in the chains of servile obedience and allows everyone the utmost freedom of action. In this respect he is quite refreshingly different from most of the teachers and *yogis* I have met in India.

My meditations take the line he had indicated during my first visit, when he had tantalised me by the vagueness which seemed to surround many of his answers. I have begun to look into my own self.

Who am I?

Am I this body of flesh, blood and bone?

Am I the mind, the thoughts and the feelings which distinguish me from every other person?

One has hitherto naturally and unquestioningly accepted the affirmative answers to these questions but the Maharshi has warned me not to take them for granted. Yet he has refused to formulate any systematic teaching. The gist of his message is:

"Pursue the enquiry 'Who am I?' relentlessly. Analyse your entire personality. Try to find out where the I-thought begins. Go on with your meditations. Keep turning your attention within. One day the wheel of thought will slow down and an intuition will mysteriously arise. Follow that intuition, let your thinking stop, and it will eventually lead you to the goal."

I struggle daily with my thoughts and cut my way slowly into the inner recesses of mind. In the helpful proximity of the Maharshi, my meditations and self soliloquies become increasingly less tiring and more effective. A strong expectancy and sense of being guided inspire my constantly repeated efforts. There are strange hours when I am clearly conscious of the unseen power of the Sage being powerfully impacted on my mentality, with the result that I penetrate a little deeper still into the shrouded borderland of being which surrounds the human mind.

The close of every evening sees the emptying of the hall as the Sage, his disciples and visitors adjourn for supper to the dining room. As I do not care for their food and will not trouble to prepare my own, I usually remain alone and await their return. However, there is one item of the hermitage diet which I find attractive and palatable, and that is curds. The Maharshi, having discovered my fondness for it, usually asks the cook to bring me a cupful of the drink each night.

About half an hour after their return, the inmates of the hermitage, together with those visitors who have remained, wrap themselves up in sheets or thin cotton blankets and retire to sleep on the tiled floor of the hall. The Sage himself uses his divan as a bed. Before he finally covers himself with the white sheets his faithful attendant thoroughly massages his limbs with oil.

I take up a glazed iron lantern when leaving the hall and set out on my lonely walk to the hut. Countless fireflies move amongst flowers and plants and trees in the garden compound. Once, when I am two or three hours later than usual and midnight is approaching, I observe these strange insects put out their weird lights. Often they are just as numerous among the thick growths of bush and cactus through which I have later to pass. One has to be careful not to tread on scorpions or snakes in the dark. Sometimes the current of meditation has seized me so profoundly that I am unable and unwilling to stop it, so that I pay little heed to the narrow path of lighted ground upon which I walk. And so I retire to my modest hut, close the tightly fitting heavy door, and draw the shutters over glassless windows to keep out unwelcome animal intruders. My last glimpse is of a thicket of palm trees which stands on one side of my clearing in the bush, the silver moonlight coming in streams over their interlaced feathery tops.

Tablets of Forgotten Truth

MY PEN WOULD WANDER ON INTO SOME account of the scenic life around me, and into further record of many talks with the Maharshi, but it is now time to draw the chronicle to a close.

I study him intently and gradually come to see in him the child of a remote Past, when the discovery of spiritual truth was reckoned of no less value than is the discovery of a gold mine today. It dawns upon me with increasing force that, in this quiet and obscure corner of South India, I have been led to one of the last of India's spiritual supermen. The serene figure of this living Sage brings the legendary figures of his country's ancient *rishis* nearer to me. One senses that the most wonderful part of this man is withheld. His deepest soul, which one instinctively recognises as being loaded with rich wisdom, eludes one. At times he still remains curiously aloof, and at other times the kindly benediction of his interior grace binds me to him with hoops of steel. I learn to submit to the enigma of his personality, and to accept him as I find him. But if humanly speaking, he is well insulated against outside contacts, whoever discovers the requisite Ariadne's thread can walk the inner path leading to spiritual contact with him. And I like him greatly because he is so simple and modest, when an atmosphere of authentic greatness lies so palpably around him; because he makes no claims to occult powers and heirophantic knowledge to impress the mystery loving nature of his countrymen, and because he is so totally without any traces of pretension that he strongly resists every effort to canonise him during his lifetime.

It seems to me that the presence of men like the Maharshi ensures the continuity down history of a divine message from regions not easily accessible to us all. It seems to me, further, that one must accept the fact that such a Sage comes to reveal something to us, not to argue anything with us. At any rate, his teachings make a strong appeal to me, for his personal attitude and practical method, when understood, are quite scientific in their way. He brings in no supernatural power and demands no blind religious faith. The sublime spirituality of the Maharshi's atmosphere and the rational self-questioning of his philosophy find but a faint echo in yonder temple. Even the word "God" is rarely on his lips. He avoids the dark and debatable waters of wizardry, in which so many promising voyages have ended in shipwreck. He simply puts forward a way of self-analysis, which can be practised irrespective of any ancient or modern theories and beliefs which one may hold, a way that will finally lead man to true self-understanding.

I follow this process of self-divestment in the effort to arrive at pure integral being. Again and again I am aware that the Maharshi's mind is imparting something to my own, though no words may be passing between us. The shadow of impending departure hangs over my efforts, yet I spin out my stay until bad health takes a renewed hand in the game and accelerates an irrevocable decision to go. Indeed, out of the deep inner urgency which drew me here, has come enough will power to overthrow the plaints of a tired sick body and a weary brain and to enable me to maintain residence in this hot static air. But Nature will not be defeated for long and before long a physical breakdown becomes threateningly imminent. Spiritually my life is nearing its peak, but — strange paradox! — physically it is slipping downwards to a point lower than it has hitherto touched. For a few hours before the arrival of the culminating experience of my contact with the Maharshi, I start to shiver violently and perspire with abnormal profuseness — intimations of coming fever.

I return hastily from an exploration of some usually veiled sanctuaries of the great temple and enter the hall when the evening meditation period has run out half its life. I slip quietly to the floor and straightway assume my regular meditation posture. In a few seconds I compose myself and bring all wandering thoughts to a strong centre. An intense interiorization of consciousness comes with the closing of eyes.

The Maharshi's seated form floats in a vivid manner before my mind's eye. Following his frequently repeated instruction I endeavour to pierce through the mental picture into that which is formless, his real being and inner nature, his soul. To my surprise the effort meets with almost instantaneous success and the picture disappears again, leaving me with nothing more than a strongly felt sense of his intimate presence.

The mental questionings which have marked most of my earlier meditations have lately begun to cease. I have repeatedly interrogated my consciousness of physical, emotional and mental sensations in turn, but, dissatisfied in the quest of Self, have eventually left them all. I have then applied the attention of consciousness to its own centre, striving to become aware of its place of origin. Now comes the supreme moment. In that concentration of stillness, the mind withdrawn into itself, one's familiar world begins to fade off into shadowy vagueness. One is apparently environed for a while by sheer nothingness, having arrived at a kind of mental blank wall. And one has to be as intense as possible to maintain one's fixed attention. But how hard to leave the lazy dalliance of our surface life and draw the mind to a pin-point of concentration!

Tonight I flash swiftly to this point, with barely a skirmish against the continuous sequence of thoughts which usually play the prelude to its arrival. Some new and powerful force comes into dynamic action within my inner world and bears me inwards with resistless speed. The first great battle is over, almost without a stroke, and a pleasurable, happy, easeful feeling succeeds its high tension.

In the next stage I stand apart from the intellect, conscious that it is thinking, but warned by an intuitive voice that it is merely an instrument. I watch these thoughts with a weird detachment. The power to think, which has hitherto been a matter for merely ordinary pride, now becomes a thing from which to escape, for I perceive with startling clarity that I have been its unconscious captive. There follows the sudden desire to stand outside the intellect and just *be*. I want to dive into a place deeper than thought. I want to know what it will feel like to deliver myself from the constant bondage of the brain, but to do so with all my attention awake and alert.

It is strange enough to be able to stand aside and watch the very action of the brain as though it were someone else's, and to see how thoughts take their rise and then die, but it is stranger still to realize intuitively that one is about to penetrate into the mysteries which hide in the innermost recesses of man's soul. I feel like some Columbus about to land on an uncharted continent. A perfectly controlled and subdued anticipation quietly thrills me.

But how to divorce oneself from the age-old tyranny of thoughts? I remember that the Maharshi has never suggested that I should attempt to force the stoppage of thinking. "Trace thought to its place of origin," is his reiterated counsel, "watch for the real Self to reveal itself, and then your thoughts will die down of their own accord." So, feeling that I have found the birthplace of thinking, I let go of the powerfully positive attitude which has brought my attention to this point and surrender myself to complete passivity, yet still keeping as intently watchful as a snake of its prey.

This poised condition reigns until I discover the correctness of the Sage's prophecy. The waves of thought naturally begin to diminish. The workings of logical rational sense drops towards zero point. The strangest sensation I have experienced till now grips me. Time seems to reel dizzily as the antennae of my rapidly growing intuition begin to reach out into the unknown. The reports of my bodily senses are no longer heard, felt, remembered. I know that at any moment I shall be standing *outside* things, on the very edge of the world's secret.

Finally it happens. Thought is extinguished like a snuffed candle. The intellect withdraws into its real ground, that is, consciousness working unhindered by thoughts. I perceive what I have suspected for sometime and what the Maharshi has confidently affirmed, that the mind takes its rise in a transcendental source. The brain has passed into a state of complete suspension as it does in deep sleep, yet there is not the slightest loss of consciousness. I remain perfectly calm and fully aware of who I am and what is occurring. Yet my sense of awareness has been drawn out of the narrow confines of the separate personality; it has turned into something sublimely all embracing. Self still exists, but it is a changed, radiant self. For something that is far superior to the unimportant personality which *was* I, some deeper, diviner being rises into consciousness and *becomes* me. With it arrives an amazing new sense of absolute freedom, for thought is like a loom-shuttle which always is going to and fro, and to be freed from its tyrannical motion is to step out of prison into the open air.

I find myself outside the rim of world consciousness. The planet, which has so far harboured me, disappears. I am in the midst of an ocean of blazing light. The latter, I feel rather than think, is the primeval stuff out of which worlds are created, the first state of matter. It stretches away into untellable infinite space, incredibly *alive*.

I touch, as in a flash, the meaning of this mysterious universal drama which is being enacted in space, and then return to the primal point of being. I, the new I, rest in the lap of holy bliss. I have drunk the Platonic Cup of Lethe, so that yesterday's bitter memories and tomorrow's anxious cares have disappeared completely. I have attained a divine liberty and an almost indescribable felicity. My arms embrace all creation with profound sympathy, for I understand in the deepest possible way that to know all is not merely to pardon all, but to love all. My heart is remoulded in rapture.

How shall I record these experiences through which I next pass, when they are too delicate for the touch of my pen? Yet the starry truths which I learn may be translated into the language of earth, and will not be a vain one. So I seek, all too roughly, to bring back some memorials of the wonderful archaic world which stretches out, untracted and unpathed, behind the human mind.

§

Man is grandly related, and a greater Being suckled him than his mother. In his wiser moments he may come to know this.

Once, in the far days of his own past, man took an oath of lofty allegiance and walked, turbaned in divine grandeur, with gods. If today the busy world calls to him with imperious demand and he gives himself up to it, there are those who have not forgotten his oath and he shall be reminded of it at the appropriate hour.

There is that in man which belongs to an imperishable race. He neglects his true Self almost completely, but his neglect can never affect or alter its shining greatness. He may forget it and entirely go to sleep in the senses, yet on the day when it stretches forth its hand and touches him, he shall remember who he is and recover his soul.

Man does not put true value upon himself because he has lost the divine sense. Therefore, he runs after another man's opinion, when he could find complete certitude more surely in the spiritually authoritative centre of his own being. The Sphinx surveys no earthly landscape. Its unflinching gaze is always directed inwards, and the secret of its inscrutable smile is Self-knowledge.

He who looks within himself and perceives only discontent, frailty, darkness and fear, need not curl his lip in mocking doubt. Let him look deeper and longer, deeper and longer, until he presently becomes aware of faint tokens and breath-like indications which appear when the heart is still. Let him heed them well, for they will take life and grow into high thoughts that will cross the threshold of his mind like wandering angels, and these again shall become forerunners of a voice which will come later — the voice of a hidden, recondite and mysterious being who inhabits his centre, who is his own ancient Self.

The divine nature reveals itself anew in every human life, but if a man walks indifferently by, then the revelation is as seed on stony ground. No one is excluded from this divine consciousness; it is man who excludes himself. Men make formal and pretentious enquiry into the mystery and meaning of life, when all the while each bird perched upon a green bough, each child holding its fond mother's hand, has solved the riddle and carries the answer in its face. That Life, which brought you to birth, O Man, is nobler and greater than your farthest thought; believe in its beneficent intention towards you and obey its subtle injunctions whispered to your heart in half-felt intuitions.

The man who thinks he may live as freely as his unconsidered desires prompt him and yet not carry the burden of an eventual reckoning, is binding his life to a hollow dream. Whoever sins against his fellows or against himself pronounces his own sentence thereby. He may hide his sins from the sight of others, but he cannot hide them from the all-recording eyes of the gods. Justice still rules the world with inexorable weight, though its operations are often unseen and though it is not always to be found in stone built courts of law. Whoever escapes from paying the legal penalties of earth can never escape from paying the just penalties which the gods impose. Nemesis — remorseless and implacable — holds such a man in jeopardy every hour.

Those who have been held under the bitter waters of sorrow, those who have moved through shadowed years in the mist of tears, will be somewhat readier to receive the truth which life is ever silently voicing. If they can perceive nothing else, they can perceive the tragical transience which attends the smiles of fortune. Those who refuse to be deluded by their brighter hours will not suffer so greatly from their darker ones. There is no life that is not made up of the warp of pleasure and the woof of suffering. Therefore, no man can afford to walk with proud and pontifical air. He who does so takes his perambulation at a grave peril. For humility is the only befitting robe to wear in the presence of the unseen gods, who may remove in a few days what has been acquired during many years. The fate of all things moves in cycles and only the thoughtless observer can fail to note this fact. Even in the universe it may be seen that every perihelion is succeeded by an aphelion. So in the life and fortunes of man, the flood of prosperity may be succeeded by the ebb of privation, health may be a fickle guest, while love may come only to wander again. But when the night of protracted agony dies, the dawn of newfound wisdom glimmers. The last lesson of these things is that the eternal refuge in man, unnoticed and unsought as it may be, must become what it was once — his solace, or disappointment and suffering will periodically conspire to drive him in upon it. No man is so lucky that the gods permit him to avoid these two great tutors of the race.

A man will feel safe, protected, secure, only when he discovers that the radiant wings of sublimity enfold him. While he persists in remaining unillumined, his best inventions shall become his worst impediments, and everything that draws him closer to the material frame of things shall become another knot he must later untie. For he is inseparably allied to his ancient past, he stands always in the presence of his inner divinity and cannot shake it off. Let him, then, not remain unwitting of this fact but deliver himself, his worldly cares and secret burdens, into the beautiful care of his better self and it shall not fail him. Let him do this, if he would live with gracious peace and die with fearless dignity.

He who has once seen his real Self will never again hate another. There is no sin greater than hatred, no sorrow worse than the legacy of lands splashed with blood which it inevitably bestows, no result more certain than that it will recoil on those who send it forth. Though none can hope to pass beyond their sight, the gods themselves stand unseen as silent witnesses of man's lawful handiwork. A moaning world lies in woe all around them, yet sublime peace is close at hand for all; weary men, tried by sorrow and torn by doubts, stumble and grope their way through the darkened streets of life, yet a great light beats down upon the paving stones before them. Hate will pass from the world only when man learns to see the faces of his fellows, not merely by the ordinary light of day, but by the transfiguring light of their divine possibilities; when he can regard them with the reverence they deserve as the faces of beings in whose hearts dwells an element akin to that Power which men name God.

All that is truly grand in Nature and inspiringly beautiful in the arts speaks to man of himself. Where the priest has failed his people the illumined artist takes up his forgotten message and procures hints of the soul for them. Whoever can recall rare moments when beauty made him a dweller amid the eternities should, whenever the world tires him, turn memory into a spur and seek out the sanctuary within. Thither he should wander for a little peace, a flush of strength and glimmer of light, confident that the moment he succeeds in touching his true Selfhood he will draw infinite support and find perfect compensation. Scholars may burrow like moles among the growing piles of modern books and ancient manuscripts which line the walls of the house of learning but they can learn no deeper secret than this, no higher truth than the supreme truth that man's very Self is divine. The wistful hopes of man may wane as the years pass, but the hope of undying life, the hope of perfect love, and the hope of assured happiness, shall ultimately find a certain fulfilment; for they constitute prophetic instincts of an ineluctable destiny which can in no way be avoided.

The world looks to ancient prophets for its finest thoughts and cringes before dusty eras for its noblest ethics. But when a man receives the august revelation of his own starry nature he is overwhelmed. All that is worthy in thought and feeling now comes unsought to his feet. Inside the cloistral quiet of his mind arise visions not less sacred than those of the Hebrew and Arab seers who reminded their race of its divine source. By this same auroral light Buddha understood and brought news of Nirvana to men. And such is the all-embracing love which this understanding awakens, that Mary Magadalene wept out her soiled life at the feet of Jesus.

No dust can ever settle on the grave grandeur of these ancient truths, though they have lain in time since the early days of our race. No people has ever existed but has also received intimations of this deeper life which is open to man. Whoever is ready to accept them must not only apprehend these truths with his intelligence, until they sparkle among his thoughts like stars among the asteroids but must appropriate them with his heart until they inspire him to diviner action.

§

I return to this mundane sphere impelled by a force which I cannot resist. By slow unhurried stages I become aware of my surroundings. I discover that I am still sitting in the hall of the Maharshi and that it is apparently deserted. My eyes catch sight of the hermitage clock and I realize that the inmates must be in the dining room at their evening meal. And then I become aware of someone on my left. It is the seventy-five year old former station-master, who is squatting close beside me on the floor with his gaze turned benevolently on me.

"You have been in a spiritual trance for nearly two hours," he informs me. His face, seamed with years and lined with old cares, breaks into smiles as though he rejoices in my own happiness.

I endeavour to make some reply, but discover to my astonishment that my power of speech has gone. Not for almost fifteen minutes do I recover it. Meanwhile the old man supplements the further statement.

"The Maharshi watched you closely all the time. I believe his thoughts guided you."

When the Sage returns to the hall, those who follow him take up their position for the short interval which precedes the final retirement for the night. He raises himself up on the divan and crosses his legs; then, resting an elbow on the right thigh, he holds his chin within the upright hand, two fingers covering his cheek. Our eyes meet across the intervening space and he continues to look intently at me.

And when the attendant lowers the wicks of the hall's lamps, following the customary nightly practice I am struck once again by the strange lustre in the Maharshi's calm eyes. They glow like twin stars through the half darkness. I remind myself that never have I met in any man eyes as remarkable as those of this last descendant of India's *rishis*. In so far as the human eyes can mirror divine power, it is a fact that the Sage's do that.

The heavily scented incense smoke rises in soft spirals the while I watch those eyes that never flicker. During the forty minutes which pass so strangely, I say nothing to him and he says nothing to me. What use are words? We now understand each other better without them, for in this profound silence our minds approach a beautiful harmony, and in this optic telegraphy I receive a clear unuttered message. Now that I have caught a wonderful and memorable glimpse of the Maharshi's viewpoint on life, my own inner life has begun to mingle with his.

§

I fight the oncoming fever during the two days which follow and manage to keep it at bay.

The old man approaches my hut in the afternoon.

"Your stay among us draws to an end, my brother," he says regretfully. "But you will surely return to us one day?"

"Most surely!" I echo confidently.

When he leaves me I stand at the door and look up at the Hill of the Holy Beacon — Arunachala, the Sacred Red Mountain, as the people of the countryside prefer to call it.

It has become the colourful background of all my existence; always I have but to raise my eyes from whatever I am doing, whether eating, walking, talking or meditating, and there is its strange, flat headed shape confronting me in the open or through a window. It is somehow inescapable in this place, but the strange spell it throws over me is more inescapable still. I begin to wonder whether this queer, solitary peak has enchanted me. There is a local tradition that it is entirely hollow and that in its interior dwell several great spiritual beings who are invisible to mortal gaze, but I disdain the story as a childish legend. And yet this lonely hill holds me in a powerful thrall, despite the fact that I have seen others, infinitely more attractive. This rugged piece of Nature, with its red laterite boulders tumbled about in disorderly masses and glowing like dull fire in the sunlight, possesses a strong personality which emanates a palpable awe creating influence.

With the fall of dusk I take my farewells of everyone except the Maharshi. I feel quietly content because my battle for spiritual certitude has been won, and because I have won it without sacrificing my dearly held rationalism for a blind credulity. Yet when the Maharshi comes to the courtyard with me a little later, my contentment suddenly deserts me. This man has strangely conquered me and it deeply affects my feelings to leave him. He has grappled me to his own soul with unseen hooks which are harder than steel, although he has sought only to restore a man to himself, to set him free and not to enslave him. He has taken me into the benign presence of my spiritual Self and helped me, dull Westerner that I am, to translate a meaningless term into a living and blissful experience.

I linger over parting, unable to express the profound emotions which move me. The indigo sky is strewn with stars, which cluster in countless thousands close over our heads. The rising moon is a thin crescent disc of silver light. On our left the evening fireflies are making the compound grove radiant, and above them the plumed heads of tall palms stand out in black silhouette against the sky.

My adventure in self-metamorphosis is over, but the turning axle of time will bring me back to this place, I know. I raise my palms and close them together in the customary salutation and then mutter a brief goodbye. The Sage smiles and looks at me fixedly, but says not a word.

One last look towards the Maharshi, one last glimpse by dim lantern light of a tall copper-skinned figure with lustrous eyes, another farewell gesture on my part, a slight wave of his right hand in response, and we part.

I climb into the waiting bullock cart, the driver swishes his whip, the obedient creatures turn out of the courtyard into the rough pate and then trot briskly away into the jasmine-scented tropic night.

* * *